Paul Norton

The Breath Of Life

an autobiography of a medium

LIVING WORLD

Copyright © Paul Norton 1995
First published in Great Britain in 1995 by
Living World Publications

All rights reserved. No part of this publication
may be reproduced in any form or by any means -
graphic, electronic, or mechanical, including
photocopying, recording, taping or information
storage and retrieval systems - without the prior
permission in writing of the publisher

British Library Cataloguing in Publication Data.
A catalogue record for this book is available from
the British Library

ISBN 0 952646 90 0

LIVING WORLD PUBLICATIONS
PO BOX 177
DONCASTER
SOUTH YORKSHIRE
DN5 9XA

Dedicated to all of those people, in both worlds who have offered their very best for very little most especially my dear friend Daz, without whom this would not have been possible.................

'Death is but a temporary parting.'

The Breath Of Life

Foreword

It is vitally important that younger mediums are prepared to take over from us older ones and I have spent many years working towards this end. Many are now working in the movement.

I am absolutely delighted that there are dedicated sensitives like Paul Norton who are ready to carry on helping those in need.

Having seen him work, I am quite sure that he will be one of the very best of the young mediums.

This book will serve as an introduction to a brilliant young man and I would like to take this opportunity to wish Paul every success with his first book and a long and happy life for the future.

> Doris Collins
> Willen Village 1995

Introduction

A lot has happened in a comparatively short space of time. My life was similar to that of any other nineteen year old. I had a good job, with prospects, a large circle of friends, with whom I would often go out to the pubs and clubs, (when not working). Everything was moving quite nicely in the direction I wished it to go.

That was until one November evening, back in 1984. I didn't realize at the time, that the events which were to follow, would alter the whole course of my life and my outlook upon it.

Turning all that which I had learned over the years, around completely, into a new, more positive way of life. Proving that out of the bad things in life, true goodness can be found, along with a new tremendous knowledge that death is not the end, but the beginning of a wonderful journey into life eternal, life in another form of dimension, life in the living world beyond......

Chapter 1

I was just drifting off to sleep when there was knock at the front door. I listened carefully and soon realized that it was my brother, Tony. He wanted to collect some blankets because he and some friends were sleeping out in their van.

As he came rushing up the stairs I heard him say that Paul, who was a friend of his and the family, had been involved in an accident. He quickly collected the blankets and rushed down stairs. Just as he was going back out, mum shouted,
'How is he?'
'He's dead,' came Tony's reply as he slammed the door.

We all knew Paul quite well and this came as a tremendous shock. As the story unfolded it turned out that Paul and some friends had gone off to Skegness for the weekend, on their motor bikes. On the way through Gainsborough, they'd come across a very bad bend. Apparently, Paul had lost control of his bike and both he and Mick, his passenger, came off the machine.

The momentum had taken them sliding down the road and into the path of an on coming car. Paul was killed instantly and Mick received quite bad injuries to his legs.

A strange thing happened afterwards. Whilst Mick was in hospital recovering from his injuries he'd apparently told some visitors that Paul had been to see him on the evening of the accident. At the time, the Doctors had thought it best not to tell Mick that Paul had been killed. So he had no idea Paul had passed away and yet he was perfectly sure he'd seen him.
Some people obviously thought that Mick had imagined it, what with the shock and trauma involved. But I, along with others tended to think differently. We

really believed that Paul had been to see Mick, after all, they were good friends. And surely he'd want to make sure that Mick was alright? In any case, choose whatever anyone thought, Mick still insisted that Paul had visited him.

I'd never really been close to anyone who'd died before and so I didn't know the feelings that people usually experienced. I remember there being a wave of pain that seemed to go through my whole body and mind. It was kind of like a massive tooth ache, except the pain was spreading all over.

Upon reflection, at the time I found it so difficult to accept, that one minute a person could be alive and full of vitality and the next 'dead' and gone. Somehow deep inside, I seemed to know that it wasn't possible.

I couldn't in any shape or form, no matter how hard I tried, accept that death was the end. My thoughts and feelings certainly told me something quite different.

Surely, all of the learning and teaching that we go through in life must be a kind of preparation for something far greater than what we could ever imagine? Otherwise what would be the point of learning continuously for it all to come to an abrupt end at some time, be it sooner or later?

It wasn't just 'death' that I hadn't experienced, I'd never seen a dead body either. The thought of it all petrified me. I had these horrific visions to mind. I was encouraged to go and see Paul and so for 'safety' I went along with my brother and his girlfriend and a couple of other people.

At the chapel of rest, everyone commented on how Paul looked so different. At a first glance, you'd have thought that he was asleep. Yet there was something missing, that personality that we all knew wasn't there, even though the physical body was.

It seemed as if Paul had moved to one side, you know, as if he was there but not there, if you understand what I mean? To be honest, it all felt rather strange. We were standing there, expecting him to wake and sit up at any moment. We were talking quietly, as if not to disturb him. Our whole personalities seemed to alter into a slow motion type of dreamy state.

The funeral was a very sad affair. Hundreds turned up at the crematorium to pay their respects. The chapel was full and so were the corridors alongside it, which overlooked a small fountain that we could see through the large glass windows. Despite the crowd, there was an unearthly silence, except for the trickle of water from the fountain.

The service only appeared to last a few minutes after which the curtains at the altar began to slowly close. At this point everyone became so overwhelmed with grief. No one was able to comprehend the tragic loss of such a young life. Paul's mother was absolutely devastated.

We were all invited back to the house, for a drink afterwards. There were so many people, that some had to stand in the driveway.

Each time that Paul's mother approached us, we would give a brief smile and slightly bow our heads, as it became increasingly difficult to know exactly what to say. After all, what on earth could we say to a mother who had just lost a child so tragically? She would give a distant, vacant smile in return, one which seemed to sum up the whole situation. A sort of look that said 'this cannot be happening to me.'

I visited Paul's mother as much as possible after the funeral, because I knew that this would be the time when she needed people the most. The time when everyone else had gone back to their homes and own lives.

As expected, Paul became the centre of conversation. Both his mother and I would talk endlessly about the funny and sad times surrounding his short and yet action packed life. She kept the memories of him alive and would often say that she could feel his presence around her, standing by her side. I was in agreement with her, somehow knowing that what she was saying was perfectly true. At that time it was a very much needed and comforting thought to feel as if we were being watched over by Paul.

A short time later, whilst on my way home from work one evening. I came across an advertisement in the local paper. I couldn't really fail to notice it. In large green letters plastered across the page, it said, 'Doris Collins, A Woman Of Spirit.'

I read the article that accompanied a full length photograph of a somewhat mysterious looking Doris Collins in an equally mysterious green flowing gown, which seemed to have an eerie aura about it.

It explained that Doris, who was a spiritualist medium and healer, would be passing on messages from the 'otherside' and giving spiritual healing to audience members at a special meeting at the Odeon in Doncaster. Intrigued by it all and taken aback by the photo, I decided that I would like to go along and see what it was all about.

When I got home I gave Paul's mother a call and told her about the advert, whilst asking her if she fancied going along. She was so obviously desperate that she jumped at the chance immediately.   I quickly cut the call short, so as not to waste time and telephoned the odeon to book the tickets. Much to my surprise we got the last two, which were separate seats, out of one thousand and the meeting wasn't for another six weeks!

When they arrived, I put the tickets in my diary, checking them often to make sure that they were still there. Almost as if I feared I would lose or misplace them.

I continued to visit Paul's mother at least a couple of times a week, to see how she was and of course chat about Paul and times gone by, as well as talk of the meeting that we had bought tickets for, looking forward to it.

We had another month or so to wait and yet it seemed like an eternity passing by very slowly as with most of the things that we tend to look forward to in life!

About three weeks before the meeting, Dad had to go into hospital. It wasn't so much a physical illness, but more of an emotional one.

You see he'd been out of work for quite some time and this amongst other things had caused him to become depressed. Adding to that Paul's death, he really felt as if he just couldn't cope any more.

It was a difficult time for Dad, which of course made it the same for all of us. If it wasn't one thing upsetting, or going wrong, it was another. We all tried to keep things ticking over as smoothly as we could.

Dad had been in hospital for a couple of weeks, when his Doctor felt that he was much better and he should come back home. He didn't really want to at that stage, but with some encouragement from the nursing staff, he reluctantly agreed.

I didn't really get to see much of him because I worked a late shift in a night club and so was out until the early hours of the morning. Often sleeping in for the best part of the following day. And on Sundays most of the staff at work would go out together to a club which opened late. So I seemed to have very little time and even when I did, Dad was usually out walking the dog or at the shops.

Easter Sunday was no exception. It had been a long week and so I looked forward to going out and unwinding. I didn't have any change for the bus so I decided to ask Dad if he could lend me some until the following day.

Dad had very little, so he tried to look after it. But with my charm, I managed to persuade him.

'Here,' he said with a grin, 'thirty six pence, make sure you pay it back.'

'I promise,' I replied as I was going out of the door, 'You'll get it back with interest.'

I heard Dad Laugh.

The club was packed full, so much so, that you just couldn't move at all. Afterwards, a few of my work friends were going on to an all night party. They'd asked me if I wanted to go. At first I said no, because I felt so tired and weak, with the crush, but as the evening wore on, I started to liven up more and agreed.

We had to walk about a mile from the town centre, yet despite the cold air it was well worth it. There were plenty of people, a disco, plenty of food and drink, what more could we ask for?

During the evening, Mandy, one of the bar staff from work, produced a pack of tarot cards.

'Anyone for a reading?' she said, whilst peering at our eager looking faces.

'I'll have a go,' I replied, feeling somewhat brave, as if I was just about to 'walk the plank' or something similar.

I'd heard a little bit about the tarot cards from friends at school, but I'd never had a reading nor met anyone that could use them.

Mandy asked me to shuffle the cards and then pick six from anywhere in the pack. As I shuffled away, a crowd of even more eager looking faces closed in, to form a very cramped circle. I picked out some cards and gave them back to Mandy. By this time, she was starting to look the part, with her eyes closed and her head tilted upwardly at an angle.

A few minutes went by before she opened her eyes. She seemed to fix a gaze between the cards and myself. We all joked that she was in some kind of trance. A few moments later, she started to talk whilst laying down the cards that I'd picked. Her voice appeared to have very little change to it, as if it were on one level of tone.

'There is a change at work, with your job. It is the same place but different work.' My eyes lit up, as she went on.
'You will have very little spare time. Your future is bright, you will have many children. There will be an upset at home very soon, I feel a.......'
Mandy's expression turned into a very serious frown.
'That's all I've got,' she said in her usual cheerful way.
'You stopped suddenly, why Mandy, what is it?'
'Nothing,' she said, innocently but falsely.
'Come on, you must tell me, I'm getting worried.'
Mandy paused for a few seconds,
'There is going to be a death. Now lets forget it. Who knows? I'm probably wrong,' she snapped whilst getting up and leaving the room.

It was silent for a few moments until the disc jockey, prompted by Jackie the host, played some more music. I went to the kitchen for another drink. Mandy was standing by the doorway.

'Listen Mandy, I'm sorry,' I said, 'I didn't mean to..'
Mandy stopped me in mid conversation,
'Look, Paul, it's my fault. Don't worry about it. It was only a bit of fun anyway. I don't really know how to read them, I was just having a laugh.'
I smiled and we both agreed to put the whole incident to the back of our minds.

The party continued on into the early hours of the morning, finishing at about four thirty. Everyone just crashed out where they could find a comfortable place. It was like something that you see in the comedy films, people sleeping here and there, bottles and glasses scattered around the floor, ash trays over flowing. At that time in the morning, we were all too tired to be bothered about the mess!

I'd nodded off for what I thought was just a couple of hours.

As I opened my eyes a ray of sunlight hit them and dazzled me for a few moments. I looked at my watch, it was three thirty. I stood up, quickly made myself look at least half decent and made my way over the bodies laying around, to the door. I had to be back at work for seven.

Everyone else was still sound asleep, so I opened the door slowly, and carefully closed it behind me so as not to wake anyone. Despite the sunlight, the air was quite cool, so I wrapped my coat around me and set off walking home.

I'd got about half way when I started to feel a little queasy. 'Perhaps it was the drink?' I thought. I decided to stop for a few moments and have a cigarette which only made me feel worse so I stubbed it out on the wall that I'd managed to prop myself against.

My head was still pounding to the beat of the music from the party and my stomach, by this time really was heaving. I didn't feel sick at all and yet I couldn't understand why I felt so knotted inside. It got that bad, that I decided to sit down on the floor.

Almost immediately my eyes started to get a little heavier and I felt a shudder going down my spine as my head started to spin. In an instant, I saw a picture of Dad in my mind. He appeared to be smiling. It was really strange, just like I was looking at a photograph, yet in my mind. The picture stayed there for a few moments. I blinked a couple of times to try and clear it, but it remained.

My spine was tingling all over and my stomach was even more knotted. I managed to pick myself up and started off home again. Despite still feeling dizzy, I began to walk a lot quicker. Almost as if I were in some kind of a hurry. With each minute passing, I was beginning to feel considerably worse. It was as if I was being propelled, at speed, in the direction of home.

By the time I'd reached our house I was out of breath. I stopped for a few seconds to compose myself, walked casually up the drive and then opened the back door. Mum walked into the kitchen at the same time.

In a split second thought I noticed the look on her face. It was that kind of distant haunted type of look, that I was sure I'd seen somewhere before but couldn't remember where. One that will always remain with me.
'Where have you been Paul?' she said. Before I had chance to answer mum went on,
'It's your Dad,' she paused, 'he's dead. He died this morning. We've been trying to get hold of you all day.'
I could feel my legs faltering a little, so I reached for a chair as it began to dawn on me what was happening. Dad had gone. He'd taken his own life.
To be honest, even now I cannot recall my movements or conversations around that period of time. Its as if little snippets and flashes of situations pop up in my mind as time goes on, gradually forming a clear picture of events.

This I think, happens to most of us. I wonder sometimes if it's our mind closing to what has happened and in doing so, temporarily cutting out other areas of our life as well.

I'd apparently gone to work that evening as normal, even though I still don't remember a thing about it.

Which means, I'd negotiated some of the busiest roads in Doncaster, without any thought at all, as well as collecting baskets full of glasses in an extremely busy night club and putting them through a very hot dish washing system.

I'd also had an interview for a day job and yet I cannot for the life of me remember applying for it.

I do however remember going to see Dad at the chapel of rest. In fact, I went everyday, before the funeral, to have a little private talk with him. Although I was alone, I wasn't in the least bit frightened. Not like I had been when I went to see Paul. I remember talking to him about work and things in general and occasionally, I would pause, waiting for him to respond in some way.

Part of me wanted to give Dad the hug that I hadn't given him for a long time, in fact, not since I was about twelve. The other part seemed to fear touching him, in case he sprang up and had a go at me, for some of things that I'd done wrong, as a child of which there were quite a few! My feelings were so mixed and messed up.

The funeral was the worst part. There were just close family and friends and the service was taken by a chap from the salvation army. He'd also taken Paul's funeral service and mum thought that it had been very nice.

I felt angry inside, because it didn't last very long. And this man was talking about our Dad as if he knew him, yet missing out vital important parts of his life. A whole life was talked about and over with, in twenty minutes. I wanted so much for the service to just carry on and on, without ending.

People always say that out of bad, can come good and strangely enough, at Dad's funeral, I met my Grandfather for the first time in my life. All he said to me was that I looked like my father and left it at that.

You see he was divorced from Nan and he'd never made contact with us or his own children because he feared we would let her know where he lived. She still carried a torch for him and so was often trying to get in contact, even after twenty or so years. Perhaps he felt embarrassed by this? And so he wasn't able to show his true feelings. After all, he didn't really know any of us, so it was more like meeting a colleague rather than a Grandad.

After the funeral and the customary 'wake', everyone went their own separate ways. My uncle Philip, Dad's brother, and Nan, went back to Kent and Grandad back to Durham. They all seemed to want to get back to their lives as quickly as possible. Continuing them as if nothing had happened. This was the hardest part for me.

You see all the while dad was in the chapel of rest, I had something to see, something to remember. Even during the service, there was something there that we could see, that was proof of Dad's existence. And now, all that was left, were the memories, although many happy ones, but nothing solid, or concrete. Nothing that could be touched or talked to.

I couldn't, in fact I wouldn't accept things the way they were. There just had to be something else. I was absolutely sure of it. But I just wasn't sure where to find it.

I'd almost forgotten about the psychic meeting that we'd got tickets for and it was only a couple of days away. More than ever I felt a stronger urge to go, almost as if I was being directed. It was a gut feeling I had, a kind of knowing that this was the right way to go. If there was another world, which I felt absolutely certain there was, I knew that Dad and Paul would come and talk to us, if they possibly could, so I focused my energy on the meeting.

The day couldn't arrive soon enough for me. Paul's mother picked me up at seven and we made our way to the theatre. I was clutching the tickets like no body's business making sure that I didn't lose them.

When we arrived there was a long queue around the outside of the Odeon gradually working its way inside. Everyone was talking and laughing as we took our seats. I'd never seen so many people in one room together, it was packed. The house music was soon drowned by the noise from the audience.

There was a lovely warm feeling inside of me, a feeling of calmness and peace. I'd not felt this relaxed in a long time. I glanced over to the otherside of the balcony where Paul's mother was sitting, she gave me a reassuring wave.

The lights started to dim and almost immediately there was a hushed expectant silence. Without any warning, a voice suddenly boomed over the sound system. My heart 'leapt' into my mouth.
'Ladies and Gentlemen would you please put your hands together and welcome 'A Woman of Spirit, Doris Collins...'

With that, the whole room filled with applause as Doris Collins stepped into the centre of the stage. To be honest, I wasn't really sure what I was expecting. I must say though at the time I thought that Doris seemed no different from anyone else. In fact in her opening talk, she stressed that the only difference between most of us and herself was the fact that she was more of a 'sensitive' person, able to see, feel and hear those who had passed on, or as she called them, the spirit people.

In next to no time she was picking people out of the audience, giving them messages from their 'dead' loved ones. Messages that brought a whole host of mixed feelings of both tears and laughter from everyone present. There were also frequent gasps of amazement at what was being said.

At one point, I was shocked, as Doris pointed up to the balcony where we were sitting and talked about a young lad who had been killed in a motorbike accident. The surname she gave was Paul's. I saw his mother put her hand up, along with one or two other people, but as it turned out, much to mine and Paul's mothers' disappointment, it was a message for someone else.

The feeling in the room was amazing, it had a kind of electric atmosphere, getting stronger as each message came through and this seemed to help put our disappointment aside.
Almost as quickly as it started, it was time to finish the messages and move on to spiritual healing.

Doris invited a number of people onto the stage and then proceeded to lay her hands on them. Each one had talked of a different ailment and much to everyone's surprise they said it had felt much better after the healing.
Doris then finished off with a talk on her healing, expressing her love of it after which, she closed the meeting with a simple, yet to the point prayer.

Despite being disappointed at not getting a message, I did feel considerably better. On the way out I was handed a leaflet which gave details of a local spiritualist church.
Paul's mother had already been to one and so she explained to me that it was very similar to the meeting that we had just been to only there were hymns, prayers and of course collections!

I was very interested and felt that I would have to go to the church to try and find out what I needed to know (even though I wasn't sure exactly what it was), in order to be able to understand and interpret the mixed feelings that I had about death and to help me to come to some kind of logical understanding of both life and death.

A few weeks of attempting to pluck up the courage passed by and I finally went along to College Road Spiritualist Church. I don't know why, but I was pretty scared. I think it was mainly because of the strange stories that I'd heard about the 'spook' church as some people from work had called it. As I stood outside nervously admiring the building, I took one final deep breath and walked in.

It was no different from any other church that I'd been to only of course that it was spiritualists who went along. I was given a hymn book by the lady on the door and directed to where I should sit. The room was very nicely decorated, with a platform at one end boasting a plush carpet and some beautiful looking flower arrangements.

The service began with a couple of hymns and prayers and then the medium, who was an elderly gentleman, started to give out messages, just as Doris Collins had done at the Odeon. I was sitting right at the back in the corner, slouching a little, so that I wouldn't be seen by the medium or at least I thought I wouldn't.

'I have a message for the young lad right at the back,' he said pointing in my direction.

'Me?' I replied, whilst prodding myself in the chest.

'Yes you. You have a grandfather in the spirit world who passed over with chest trouble,' he said.

As it happened, Mum's dad had passed away when I was about three. I knew he'd had something wrong with his chest so I agreed. The medium went on.

'He's telling me that you have been brought here for a reason. That reason is, that you too are a medium. You will one day travel in this country and abroad spreading the message as I and others do. You don't believe me do you?'

'Err well,' I mumbled.

By this time most of the sixty odd congregation were turning round and glaring at me and my face must have been scarlet with embarrassment.

'Well sonny,' he said, 'I am to give you one name will which be very important to you over the next two years of your life. You will remember it. This will prove to you that what we are saying is true and one day soon you will be standing here on this spot, repeating what I have been telling you, to others. The name I have to give you is, Gwyneth Williams.'

I'd never heard of a lady with that name before, but I accepted the message, mainly because I daren't do any other for the sake of saving myself further embarrassment.

After the service had finished, I made a quick exit. On the way home, feeling somewhat disappointed that neither Dad nor Paul had come to talk, I recited the message over and over in my mind. I still couldn't make head nor tail of it. It was really a little too vague for my liking.

Despite the disappointment, I'd now gotten over the initial nerves of going into the church. So I decided that I would continue to go along as often as I could, thinking that perhaps in time I would get some answers.

Because I worked such odd hours, I was only able to go, to what the church called, the Monday night open circle. This was quite different from Doris' meeting and the service that I'd been to.
Instead of there being just one medium, there were quite a few. All of them gathered around in a large

circle along with everyone else. Every now and again, a medium would stand up and give a message out.

My luck must have been in because each meeting I went to, I was given a message similar to the one that I had received at the service. The only exception to the messages were, that they were apparently coming from the medium's spirit guides, as they called them, as opposed to any relative or friend of mine.

These messages were all telling me the same thing, that I too would become a working medium, travelling many miles and appearing in front of many people. It's really strange because these were the only things I was ever told.

There were no messages from Dad or Paul, or anyone else I knew for that matter. No words of comfort or joy like I was seeking. These messages were not what I was looking for. To be honest, at times I was disheartened and there came a point when I was beginning to question the existence of this spirit world.

Still, despite all the odds I continued to have the strong feelings inside of me knowing that I should follow what I was feeling and continue in this direction.

It wasn't long before I became a regular visitor to the church and a lady, who has since become a dear friend, was kind enough to take me under her wing. I explained to her what had happened to Paul and Dad, and the feelings I'd had on the way home from the party, when Dad had died, and how I'd seen his picture in my mind.

Edie (as we call her), explained to me that Dad had obviously tried to get through to me, to let me know he had passed away and that he was alright on the otherside.

I went on to tell her about the messages I'd received. She explained to me what was taking place and tried to

interpret some of the messages that I'd told her about. She said that I was obviously a natural.
'Natural what?' I asked.
'Medium of course,' she replied whilst laughing.

As time passed, Edie taught me how to meditate and how to talk with the spirit people,
'Just talk to them like you do anyone else,' she would say, 'And in time they will answer you.'
I soon started to get the pictures in my mind, like when I'd seen Dad.

Through Edie I was able to understand their meaning. She taught me how to use the third eye, as she called it, the eye of the mind. She showed me how to interpret the pictures and feelings that I had.
Each week became a totally new experience. My mind started to function in ways that I never knew were possible. I hadn't heard any voices or really seen anything of what I would call substance, but, Edie insisted I was developing and at the right pace as well.

She eventually suggested that I should join a medium's teaching group, which she told me would help me to develop a lot better. Because a medium would teach me how to find and use the gifts properly.
'Can't you teach me?' I asked her.
'I'm not a medium,' came her reply.
Yet I'd seen Edie give what appeared to be good messages to people in the group at church and I'd heard her give some sound advice.

I didn't believe I had any gifts, but went along with Edie, more so I think, for comfort and strength. I'd only ever gone to church to see if there were any messages from my loved ones and here I was starting to receive thoughts and feelings, for other people, and now being told to join a medium's developing group.
I just didn't understand it at all. I was certainly no medium or psychic, or so I thought and to be honest I wasn't sure whether or not I wanted to be.

I went along with what was happening with the thought to mind that perhaps Dad and Paul would eventually come through with a message to me directly.

Edie introduced me to two friends of hers, Sandy and Len Jones. They told me that Edie thought I would make a promising student and so they asked me if I wanted to join their developing group. I gratefully accepted in the hope that I would make some kind of contact, with those who were dear to me.

Sandy said that it would be rather like a teaching class where the leader, herself, would teach us how to receive spirit messages. The rest of it would then be up to ourselves. She explained that she wouldn't be able to make it happen for us, but she would be able to show us the way.

Both Sandy and Len emphasized the need for me to be punctual, interested and above all, disciplined in my approach towards the group and any development.

It was arranged that the group would meet every Tuesday evening at Sandy and Len's house. The circle was to start at seven thirty, but they did say that I would be more than welcome to go along earlier if I wished. In fact, they suggested that it would be better for me to do so, to give me chance to relax before starting.

Although a little unsure, I felt quite happy going along to the group and offering them, anything that I had, in the way of knowledge, companionship or experience.

I didn't think for one moment that I would be able to do any more than just that. And for me, it would be a chance to take my mind off the things that had recently taken place.

Chapter 2

I had a hectic day ahead of me. First I had to get up early to go to work and collect my wages, because they'd forgotten to pay them into my bank account, I'd then promised mum that I would get some shopping for her. My books were due back at the library, I'd promised a sick friend I would go and visit, I had to enrol for the course I was starting at college, then I had to get back home, have my tea, have a bath and get to Sandy and Len's.

I didn't have chance to think about the developing group and I certainly didn't think I would make it in time.

It was the first night and I remember Sandy suggesting that I should try and have a relaxing day, so that I would be prepared for the group. 'Some chance,' I thought. After everything you could think of possibly going wrong, I eventually managed to get finished in time and set off for Sandy's.

The bus journey was long enough for me to use it as an opportunity to relax. Although by this time, I was feeling both nervous and excited, wondering what was going to take place. I closed my eyes for a few minutes to try and calm my thoughts. It was no use, I just kept getting flashes of different things, had I remembered this, had I remembered that, all going through my mind. The bus rocking from side to side wasn't much help either. I was struggling so much to blank everything out, that I nearly missed my stop.

I could see Len standing in the doorway, as I got near to the house.
'We thought you'd changed your mind,' he shouted, loud enough for all of the street to hear. Part of me wished I had.

The rest of the people had already arrived. Sandy introduced me to them.
'This is Pauline,' she said, 'Gary, Rosemary, David, Carol, Lilian.'

I was beginning to feel dizzy with the speed at which she had spoken.

'You can sit there Paul,' she said, pointing to a chair in the corner.
When we were all seated and relaxed, Sandy turned down the lights, said a little prayer and then asked us to follow what she was saying, in our minds, like a form of mental exercise.

She took us on a 'walk' through the countryside, up into some hills and eventually through some large golden coloured gates.
'I'm going to leave you all now for a while,' she said, 'So that you can find some inner peace.'
I drifted off quite happily with my mind filled with these beautiful thoughts. They were just like the real thing. I even thought I could feel the air in my lungs.

What only appeared to be a few minutes, was in actual fact three quarters of an hour.

'Now,' Sandy said, 'in your own time, I want you to come back to the circle, open your eyes and take a drink of water if you need one.'

One by one we brought our minds back to the circle and as our thoughts became clearer we could hear some music playing in the background. It was the theme from the film Chariots of Fire. Sandy had carefully turned up the volume on her stereo, so that the music would gradually draw us back.

I'd relaxed my mind so much so, that I could have gone to sleep right there and then. It was such a wonderful experience. I couldn't remember the last time I'd felt so good inside.

In turn, Sandy asked each one of us what, if anything, we had seen and heard. Everyone elses' story seemed so grand. They spoke of seeing and hearing people, vast colours and marvellous music. And mine, it seemed so ordinary.

'I just pictured what you were describing Sandy,' I said, somewhat uncomfortably.

'You've done well for your first time Paul,' She replied with an air of confidence. The others seemed to agree. All I'd done really, was picture the scene in my mind, 'anyone could do that,' I thought.

Despite feeling a little put out I really did enjoy the meeting. I think the fact that the other circle members supported me, had made all of the difference. I eventually convinced myself that some kind of results would come in time.

Afterwards, Sandy and Len invited both Pauline and myself to stay behind. We had a long chat about many things and Sandy was very good at explaining all about the spirit world and what it was like, and how mediums worked.

I was so enthralled by her experiences and knowledge. She gave me a book about psychic development to read and told me to be open minded about the different ways that it taught.

I discovered that Pauline lived only a couple of miles away from where I did and she kindly offered to give me a lift home and pick me up the following week. I readily accepted.

I'd been so used to relying on public transport, or my legs, that being offered a lift was a luxury. She arranged to pick me up the following Tuesday at a quarter to seven.

That evening when I got home I decided to read the book that Sandy had given to me. It was all very interesting, although at times a little bit contradictory. It described various exercises that budding students could follow to help enhance their psychic powers. Giving the most marvellous descriptions of the results of other people.

I decided to try out some of the exercises that it suggested. The first one involved visualizing a round crystal approximately a foot away from the eyes. With my mind I had to draw it nearer to me, so that it was about an inch away from my nose.

Every time I closed my eyes I could see different colours swirling around in my thoughts. I couldn't for the life of me visualize this crystal, let alone draw it nearer.

The next exercise was similar to the first only this time, I had to fill a glass bowl with water and look into it. With my eyes open I was to visualize a flower opening and then closing. All I could see, even when my eyes were perfectly relaxed was my reflection.

Over the week, I'd moved onto almost all of the exercises and by this time I was getting a little tired with them. So I decided to give the book a miss. There had been such a buzz in my mind, with all that had been happening over the weeks and all of the excitement of the circle, that I'd forgotten to get organized for college. Here I was with just a few hours left to get things done. Most of them would be spent sleeping.

I did finally manage to organize my things, finishing at about one thirty in the morning. Leaving me just a few hours to get some sleep.

The course that I was taking was in social care. It involved work experience in the caring field. Each term all of the students on the course would be going to different residential homes and schools to gain some 'hands on' experience, as well as studying the theory in college. It was a full time course lasting two years. I, like everyone else, couldn't wait to leave school and now I was going back to start learning all over again, in a similar situation!

I suppose I wasn't the only one who was nervous, but I managed to put the nerves to one side and put on a brave face, although feeling somewhat apprehensive. I set off quite early to give myself plenty of time to catch the bus and familiarise myself with my new surroundings.

High Melton was a beautiful little village and the college site was an ideal place for people to learn. There was an old church in the grounds and some of the college buildings were quite an age to. The site was on a hill and there were acres of trees and fields as far as the eye could see.

I had the letter with me which the tutor had sent, offering me a place on the course. It gave instructions on how to find the main lecture room that we would be using. All it said was that we were to meet in room GW2 underneath the library at nine o'clock.

I asked someone for directions and made my way across the site. I was just admiring the view when a cold shudder went all the way down my spine, at the same time the hairs on my arms began to stand on end. As I looked up at the library, written across the front in the largest letters possible was the familiar name, 'Gwyneth Williams Library.'

Almost immediately the words came flooding back,

'I have to give you the name Gwyneth Williams.'

It was the name that the medium had given to me the first time I'd gone to the church. He told me that the name would be very important to me for the next two years and that it would confirm his message was correct. Well I'd just started the two year course and our main lecture and registration room was underneath the Gwyneth Williams Library!

I started to believe that the medium must have been correct in what he was saying, after all, he didn't know me from Adam and I didn't even know the name until I started college. I couldn't wait to get to the circle and tell everyone what had happened. In fact I didn't, with a few minutes to spare before nine, I rushed to the phone that I'd passed on the way into the library called, Pauline and excitedly told her all about it.

As I found out later, she'd phoned around and told the whole group and so this became the talking point at the next circle.

Sandy had said that she knew exactly what the spirit world were doing and that I was to wait and see what they had in store for me. She left it at that, somewhat open ended I thought, however I trusted her completely and I fully believed in what she'd said.

That evening at the circle, we had another meditation this time, we started off on a beach sunbathing, we then went into the sea to be greeted by a couple of dolphins which took us right out and then beneath the surface going deeper and deeper until they brought us to rest in a cavern. At that point Sandy left us for forty or so minutes and then gently called us back.

The other circle members were speaking of all these things that they'd seen and done whilst in the meditation and there was me there only just managing to follow what Sandy had been saying. Yet again I felt a little disappointed, particularly after what had taken place that day concerning the message the medium had given to me.

Sandy could obviously sense this disappointment, so she took me to one side and suggested that I meditate each day for half an hour or so. She told me that it would definitely help me. I believed her and so decided I would do just that.

On the way home, I told Pauline how I'd felt at the circle. I explained to her that I couldn't understand why I'd seen many pictures and received thoughts at the church and yet at Sandy's, I didn't seem to get much at all. 'Just do what Sandy told you to,' Pauline said, 'I'll try,' I replied nodding in agreement.
The following day when I got home from college I went straight to my bedroom, closed the curtains, put on some classical music and started to meditate just as Sandy had advised.

I didn't think of anything in particular but I did notice swirling colours in my mind's eye. As they swirled and mixed in my mind I started to feel quite drowsy almost as if they were hypnotizing me. The music that I'd put on drifted into the distance and eventually as I discovered later, I'd fallen asleep.

This seemed to happen to me every night. I hadn't told anyone in the circle simply because I didn't think it was of any importance. After all, I didn't think I was the first person to fall asleep during a meditation and I was sure I wouldn't be the last. In any case I really didn't want to bother anyone with what I thought was small talk. So I continued to meditate as normal and kept quiet about sleeping.

About five or so weeks later, as usual I was meditating. The colours were soon there then the drowsy feelings and after a few moments of enjoying the colours and the feelings I immediately sensed another presence in the room. It was as if I knew who the person was even though by this time I couldn't for the life of me open my eyes.

'Mum, is that you?' I said out loud. There was no response. 'Steven, Gary, Tony,' (my brothers). There wasn't a single sound and yet I was absolutely sure there was someone there. I wasn't in the least bit frightened in fact, I was getting a little impatient with myself thinking that it was in my mind. All of a sudden right out of the blue came a very loud and clear voice.

'I am Naiomi,' said the gentle but firm voice. 'I am your guide, we've been waiting for you to come to us. We have tried so hard to get through to you but you filled your mind with your books.'

My jaw hung open in astonishment, loosely flapping trying to speak with nothing coming out.

'It has taken many months for you to understand the purpose of your life.' she added, 'I have come to tell you that all you have been told, is what we wanted you to know.'

'Oh, err,' I muttered, 'thank you.'

'But,' she continued, 'there is something more that you should know, we will be with you on the third helping you work. You must have trust in what we say and then you will see how we shall be working together. If you need to know more, just call out and we will try to be there.'
My whole mind was in a complete spin. Was I imagining it? Could it be this? Could it be that? What did she say? I was just confused and amazed.

For the next few days I seemed to go about my business in a kind of day dreamy state of mind. By the way I was acting, anyone would have thought that I was either drunk or I'd just won the pools or something like that. My mind was reliving the whole experience over and over, so I was absolutely sure what had been said.

At the next circle, I told everyone what had happened. They were just as amazed as I was.
'She told me that they would be with me on the third,' I said. Before I had chance to question what they had meant by this, Sandy interrupted the conversation.

'I have a tin here,' she said, 'there are seven straws in it. One of them is very small. Who ever picks this straw will be taking the service with me at Mexborough church next Sunday.' We all looked at each other in disbelief, as Sandy passed the tin around. Just as it was being passed to me, I felt a little skip of my heart and then came the voice again,

'It's you, but remember what I told you.'

'Paul,' said Pauline frowning a little, 'are you alright?'

'Fine,' I said somewhat vaguely.

'You look as if you've just seen a ghost,' she said chuckling.

'No,' I replied, 'I haven't seen one but I just heard one.' This brought a somewhat serious look to her face. 'The guide I told you about the other day has just spoken again. She said that it will be me and I am to remember what she told me.'

I looked at Sandy as I dipped my hand into the tin and took out a straw. She smiled at me with that kind of knowing look. Sure enough, as I was told and I'd thought, I picked the shortest straw.

'Well that settles it then,' Sandy said looking quite amused.

Later on that night, after some of the others had left, Sandy told me that she already knew I would be taking the service with her.

She went on to say that was why she had stopped me in mid conversation, because I was about to start delving and she thought that I might have spoiled her fun, by realizing what was happening. She reminded me that the date of the service was the third of November!
'Next Sunday,' she said.

Sunday soon arrived. I'd just settled my stomach down, when I heard the sound of a car horn. It was Sandy and Len. They'd come to pick me up to take me to the church. I'd been so busy with my college work all week that I hadn't given it another thought, that was until that afternoon.

I quickly checked to make sure that I looked respectable for the service, said goodbye to mum and nervously got into the car.

'Nervous Paul?' said Len with a big grin.

'I'm not going to let him know I am,' I thought,

'To be honest, I haven't really thought about it Len,' I replied innocently.

When we arrived at the church, we were shown into an ante room. It was very small and crammed with old furniture. We all just managed to squeeze in. I grappled with a couple of old chairs, until I was able to put them down just behind the door.
My stomach started to heave from side to side, it was like being on a roller coaster. I looked at Sandy for reassurance, but all she could manage was a somewhat

strained smile.

'At least I'm not on my own,' I thought.

It was one of those, 'I wish that I were some where else' situations. During that thought there came a faint knock at the door,

'Are you ready my dears?' said the kindly lady. 'I'll be chairing for you,' she added, as she lead us into the main hall.

I knew that Sandy was popular but I'd never expected to see this many people in the hall, it was so packed that people were having to stand up at the back and in the aisles. After the initial introductions, hymns and prayers, Sandy gave a philosophical talk on spiritualism. She then went on to give a very good demonstration of mediumship.

It was so good, that I was too busy watching peoples' reactions to realize what was happening next. Without any warning whatsoever, Sandy stopped her demonstration and promptly announced that I would be continuing with the service, taking her seat as she did so.

All I can remember was the churning feeling inside of me and my legs beginning to feel weak, the rest of it, is an absolute blank.

After the service had finished, a small group of people gathered around me and started to pay compliments and shake my hand. Still in a daze I just smiled, thanking them and feeling somewhat embarrassed. Sandy came up to me and put her arm around me,

'You did well Paul,' she said, 'I'm so proud of you.'
The church officials must have thought the same, because I was offered further bookings at that church

and one or two people asked me if I would take services at a couple of others. Some people even asked if I did one to one meetings, or private sittings, as they're known in the business.

I explained that I was at college full time and so at that point I didn't really have time to do them.

On the way home Sandy kept telling me how proud she was and that in no time I would get better and better with more practice.

'I'll get you some more bookings Paul,' she said.

I just smiled approvingly, despite the fact that I didn't really feel as if I was ready to take any more.

That evening, just as I was going to bed, I closed my eyes and said a little prayer of thanks, to who ever had helped me with the service and of course a little prayer for Paul and Dad. I was just enjoying those few minutes silence when my guide, Naiomi whispered to me,

'I told you that we would help. You did well because you trusted. I will speak again, with you soon, but before then you will hear about the work we have planned for you.' As quickly as the voice came through, it had disappeared.

At the circle the following week the centre point of the conversation was the service. Apparently, a couple of other circle members had gone along to watch. I didn't recall seeing any of them there. Any way, as it transpired, one of them knew one of the ladies I'd apparently given a message to. It turned out that the lady in question had lost her husband in a fire. I'd apparently told her about this, given her his name and the date that he'd passed over, along with a short comforting message.

The lady had asked if they could pass on her thanks to me for the help I'd given. It was only a small piece of information out of a thirty minute demonstration, but

36

it was as equally important to me, as it was to the lady. I'd had no idea what had taken place and at least it gave me some knowledge of the capabilities that were present and of course reassurance that I'd been able to handle the responsibility that I'd been given.

By this time, I was quite pleased with myself, but Sandy was quick to intervene,

'Always, Paul,' she said, 'remain humble.' I told Sandy that I certainly would.'

'We're running late,' she quickly added whilst switching on the cassette player. With all of the chat about the service, we'd forgotten about starting the circle. Sandy was always particular about the timing.

'We have made an agreement with the spirit world,' she would often say, adding, 'How would you like it, if they were late to help you with a service or a one to one sitting?'
It was quite true really, so in turn, within ourselves we each said a little apology to the spirit people before getting on with our meditation.

The circle carried on right up until Christmas then there was a break for the holiday. We were to start back in January.
Over the holiday, I decided to catch up on some of my college work and concentrate on my meditation. It was during this period of time, that I had the opportunity to get to know Naiomi a little bit better.

She was able to tell me that she was French Canadian, and as a child, her family moved from Canada, to Brittany France. As she grew up, she became a school teacher and eventually, she passed over when she was fifty three years old, with a heart and lung complaint. One thing about her puzzled me. She'd told me that she was a teacher and yet, even though I hadn't seen her I felt as if she was always dressed in a Nuns' habit.

I decided to ask her why I felt this.

'I always wanted to be a nun,' she told me, 'but I couldn't marry God.' She said no more in that respect and so I accepted what I had been told. Naiomi did however tell me that there was still plenty of work ahead and plenty of meditating and developing. She made it all sound so easy and yet, I knew that there would no doubt be difficulties, particularly in me being able to understand and interpret things.

I thought about a lot of things during the holidays. All of what had happened in my short life. Everything seemed as if it was starting to fit into place. I realized that I owed a great deal of thanks to both Edie, Sandy and Len for without them I knew I wouldn't have covered as much ground as I had. Of course the ultimate thank you would have to go to my dear new found friend and guide, Naiomi. She really had been a great strength to me particularly during the service that I'd taken and then the weeks afterwards, in the developing circle. At last I was starting to feel a sense of purpose, I had a goal to work towards, something very special that was close to my heart.

The holidays were soon over with and it was back to college. I had a lot of work to catch up on, but somehow managed to muddle through and meet some of the deadlines set by our tutor. The circle started up again. I'd missed it during the break even though I found myself meditating and talking to Naiomi a great deal.

I think it's because I often found it more enjoyable to be able to share the experiences of spirit activity with others, as we often did in the group. We were kind of like an extended family and this often created a secure feeling for us to be able to progress. So everything seemed to be taking its right course moving in a positive direction or at least, I thought that was the case.

One Sunday afternoon shortly after Christmas, I was just flicking through the pages of a catalogue when there came a knock at the door.

'Who could it be on a Sunday?' I thought as I went to answer it.

It was very rare for people to call round on a Sundays, mainly because most of them were likely to have still been in bed. It turned out to be Janice our next door neighbour.

'Will you tell your mother that Philip is on the phone,' she said. Philip is my uncle, Dad's brother He lived at that time in Essex. I passed the message on to mum and she went next door to take the call.

I continued to look through the catalogue when all of a sudden Naiomi interrupted my thoughts,

'It's not good,' she said, 'be prepared for the worst, but please realize we are helping her.' I was a little confused.

Mum came back looking extremely pale, 'It's your Nan,' she said 'She's dead, she died on Friday. Philip phoned to let us know, in case we saw it on the news.'

'News,' I said, still in a state of shock.

'She was murdered,' came mum's reply.

At that point I felt physically sick and ran straight to the bathroom. My blood seemed to go as cold as ice and it felt as if it was draining away. It was like some kind of dream, or rather nightmare.

First Paul, then dad and now Nan, all within twelve months. Was this really happening and if so, why? My thoughts were in a complete state of shock and I felt as if my life, again was broken into bits and pieces.

I think now it was mainly because of the way each one of them had passed. So sudden and so horrific. Maybe if they'd perhaps been ill or we were expecting them to pass, it might not have made it any easier, but I'm sure we'd have been able to take it in a little more easily.

I'd heard many people say, time and time again it's the kind of thing you read about in the paper, that you think only happens to other people. You never, for one moment expect it to happen to you, but it had.

It didn't end there though, exactly one week later, Philip telephoned again to say that his father, my Grand dad had passed away as well. He'd been suffering from cancer for some time. As I told you earlier I'd only ever met him once, and that was at Dad's funeral. It was a little sad really, that we didn't have the chance to get to know him, but unfortunately, we all think of these things, when it's too late.

A month after that mum got a letter from Australia bringing the news that one of our Aunties had passed away, she too apparently had cancer. All in all within fifteen months five people, one of whom was a family friend, yet just as close had passed away. Three of them in tragic circumstances.

Naiomi, I'm sure, helped me to keep my sanity. Being able to communicate with the spirit world didn't make it any easier, I still missed the physical presence of those who had passed over, but what it did do was instil the knowledge that one day in time I would, if I chose to, be with all of them again eternally.

The person who'd killed Nan was someone who had, over a period of time, been doing odd jobs for her. She'd apparently discovered that the young man in question had been stealing money from her. When she confronted him, he offered to pay her back. That particular day, he'd returned to her house and after some kind of disagreement he struck her head, apparently killing her instantly. It wasn't until the early hours of the morning that her body was discovered by a neighbour who had seen smoke and flames coming from Nan's kitchen from a number of fires which had been started, so it seems deliberately.

The young man was charged with manslaughter and was subsequently admitted to a secure hospital for eighteen or so months. The charge of arson, which was brought, remained on file as it was a lesser charge than manslaughter. It was such a waste of life in two respects. Firstly, Nan had been killed and secondly an eighteen year old was locked away for committing the crime. He now had to face his whole life with what he'd done, as well as the prospect of possibly not finding a good job, after his release. After all, people would surely find out eventually what had happened.

Life for us slowly started to get back to some kind of normality, even though it started to feel like this was what normality was. I felt quite sad at what had happened. I'd intended to visit Nan more often, during the summer holidays. She lived in Kent and I always looked forward to going there again and seeing her but it obviously wasn't to be.

Sadly, during this time the circle had to finish because Sandy had too many work commitments and she wasn't able to find the time to continue with it. Word had gotten around about the service I'd taken with Sandy at Mexborough and so the bookings started to flow in steadily. Although apprehensive I accepted most of them. I still had a few months to spare before I had to take my first service on my own, so I decided to start going back to the open circle at church, to get some practice in and keep my thoughts occupied.

When I'd joined Sandy's circle, I was so busy, what with college, meditating and all that had happened that I didn't have time to go to church. To be honest, I'd completely forgotten about it. Feeling somewhat guilty,

I made a firm note in my mind to go along to the next meeting.

Chapter 3

'My name is Angela,' said the voice, 'I passed with cancer. I want to thank Janet. That's her sitting over there,' she said, whilst guiding my thoughts towards a rather sad looking lady sitting awkwardly in the corner.

I'd finally gotten around to going to the church open circle. Edie was very pleased to see me. 'Hello stranger,' she said with a glint in her eye. 'We thought you'd passed on,' she added chuckling. 'Afraid not Edie, you've got me for a long time.' I was surprised to see how many people had turned up. There must have been over eighty odd. Edie told me that there was often a large group. 'It must be something in the air,' she said.

I took my seat and watched the people pour in. I noticed one lady who was obviously grief stricken and so before the circle started, I sent out a thought to the spirit world for some help for her. It turned out that this was the lady that Angela wanted to speak to.

Without hesitation I got up and walked towards her.
'I have a young lady here who tells me her name is Angela,' I said nervously. 'She says she passed with cancer and you helped to look after her, are you Janet?' The lady nodded in agreement and I soon realized that she was crying.

'Angela wants me to thank you for all of the help and love you gave to her. She says you really did put yourself out.'

'That's true,' came Janet's reply whilst dabbing her eyes.

'She must only be about twenty nine,' I said, 'and she's singing happy birthday.'

'That's right, she passed on her twenty ninth birthday.' Janet said in surprise.

That was all I had to say to Janet, so I gave her Angela's love again and sat back down.

When the circle had finished, Janet came rushing over and put her arms around me.

'Thank you, thank you so much,' she cried, 'I've been coming here for some months now and that's all I've been waiting for, thank you.' I just smiled and tried to hide my embarrassment. Janet told me that Angela was a very dear friend of hers. She went on to say that Angela had got cancer in her stomach. Because she lived alone, Janet had offered to look after her right up until the end.

'I felt guilty after she passed,' she said, 'I breathed a sigh of relief and thanked God. Ever since then I've felt so guilty and so I asked Angela to forgive me.'

I told Janet that there was no need for Angela to forgive her, because she'd helped her to pass over peacefully. Janet smiled,

'I really can't thank you enough,' she said.

Afterwards, I told Edie what Janet had said.

'You must remember that it's the spirit world who need thanking Paul, for what are you without them?' she replied. I agreed and quickly said a silent thank you.

Edie was very good at helping me to keep my feet on the ground. If ever she saw me getting above myself, she would always, extremely politely and gently remind me who I was and who I worked with.

The time to start taking the services that I had booked soon arrived. Unfortunately, there were so many, all crammed in to a few months that I didn't keep any notes on them. To be honest I can't remember anything about them either, other than being out of the house nearly every night of the week, come wind rain or sunshine and spending most of my weekends either getting my clothes ready or asking Naiomi for some help.

Because of the cost of public transport and the poor service that was generally offered, I wasn't able to take many bookings too far a field. My friends would often offer to take me to services, but I couldn't rely on them all of the time and I didn't think it would be fair for me to keep taking up their offers. Of course, I had to consider my college work as well, I still had that to do when I got back home, or during my lunch breaks. So I mainly took services in Yorkshire and continued to go to the open circle at college road.

One particular evening, I was just sitting in the corner of the school room at church, saying a little prayer, when a lady tapped me on the shoulder.'

'Paul Norton,' she said. I nodded.

'I have seen you work and I think you are very good,'

I quickly remembered what Edie had said,

'Well it's not just me, it's the spirit world as well.'

She continued,
'I was wondering if you would consider taking a charity meeting in aid of the hospital appeal? I know of a hall that can be used and I'm sure a lot of people would come along to support the event.'

'I'd love to,' I said.
Irene, as I later found out to be her name, wrote down a couple of dates for me to check and gave me her telephone number.

'I'll be in touch,' I said as she was just leaving.

I gave Irene a call the following day and we agreed a date for the meeting. She'd suggested that I went along with her to the hall to make sure that I was happy with it and decide how I wanted the layout to look. To be honest so long as I was able to see everybody without having to turn around or look straight towards my feet I was quite happy. I explained this to Irene and so instead she arranged a time for me to be picked up and taken to the meeting.

Over the following weeks, I noticed there seemed to be a kind of 'buzz' in the air. People at church would whisper and point at me. People who lived in my street seemed to give me strange looks. I couldn't fathom out what was going on. Then one day when I was in town, I'd just walked past the newspaper office when a poster caught my eye. In large bold letters it said, 'A charity evening in aid of the hospital appeal is being held at the Fairway Hotel with special guest Paul Norton the medium.' It went on to say the date, time and ticket prices.

I quickly looked around as I had this feeling of being watched. I think I was starting to get a little paranoid with this idea to mind that people would recognise me. I kept my head down and went about the rest of my business, rushing back to the bus station as quickly as I could. Now I realized why there were so many strange looks, whispers and people pointing. It didn't end there though.

The following day I got a message from Irene. Apparently the local paper wanted to do a feature on me to help create some more interest. I hadn't had much experience of the press but because it was for the hospital I thought it would be of help.

The newspaper arranged for a reporter to visit me and take down some details. Fortunately they didn't want to see me work so I didn't offer! I just answered the questions and chatted about various other topics. When the article came out I was even more embarrassed than I had been with the posters. The headline on the page read, 'Powerful Paul'! The article went on to say how I'd been gifted with special powers of clairvoyancy.

I'd never even mentioned the word powers and I certainly didn't consider myself to be gifted. With regards to clairvoyancy, they made it sound as if I was some kind of end of pier fortune teller. Although disappointed with what they'd written, I was soon able to put it to one side by the fact that the tickets were selling very fast indeed.

The evening arrived much to soon for my liking. I got to the hotel early so I could get changed and have a little rest in the small room that they'd set aside for me. As the time passed I started to wonder why I couldn't hear anything. Being nosy, I popped my head around the door of the room. I could just about make out the sound of voices, so I carefully pulled open one of the heavy doors leading to the hall. To my shock it was jam packed with people. The doors were that heavy, that they'd sound proofed the noise of the crowd. At that point I started to wish that I'd never agreed to take the meeting.

It was the first time that I was working outside of a spiritualist church. I'd gotten used to the secure confines of the open circles and weekly meetings at church and now here I was about to demonstrate to the general public.

I said prayer after prayer begging Naiomi and the spirit world for help, in between rushing in and out of the toilets. I paced the corridors doing everything I could think of to calm myself down. Eventually I went back into the small room and lit up a cigarette. I'd just started to puff on it when there came a faint knock at the door. It was Irene.

'It's time to start Paul.' She said, as nervously as I felt.

I followed Irene through to the main hall and as she opened the doors, I just caught the words, '......Paul Norton.'

As I walked up on to the platform my heart flipped a little. I soon managed to compose myself and went on to explain how it all worked and what would be happening. After which I went straight into the demonstration.

One young girl who had passed with leukemia made an emotional return to her mother and older sister. She was able to tell us both the colour and type of clothes that her mother had buried her in, they were her favourite.

'I've got my golden locks back now,' she said excitedly.

A father was reunited with two of his five daughters. Amidst the tears he was able to make a joke about one of the ladies who'd dyed her hair that afternoon. 'She should have been blonde not orange,' he said, adding, 'she didn't leave it on long enough. She should have read the instructions. She's always in a hurry.'

This caused everyone including the lady to fall into fits of giggles and laughter.

The evening just seemed to sail by and the people kept asking for more. It was a tremendous success both for the charity, the spirit world and the audience. A lot of the people stayed behind to ask questions and many wanted private sittings.

I explained that I would be able to take them when I'd finished college. Although it was some ten months away people asked if they could book in advance. Reluctantly I agreed and gave out my telephone number to those who'd asked for it.

One of the messages at the fairway meeting was for a lady called Pam and her daughter, Sally-Ann. She wrote to me afterwards

'My daughter and I attended your meeting at the Fairway Hotel a few months ago. You picked my daughter out, she was the girl sitting right towards the back of the hall.

You said that there was a man communicating, who'd been in the army and spent a lot of time in India and also France. This was her grandfather. He told you that my daughter, who you first went to, was pregnant, which she was and that he was showing you pink booties. My daughter has since had a little girl.

You spoke of the problems around her of which there were a lot and you said it would all work out. It has done. You said he was with Mary, well Mary is his first wife. You said that the lady sitting next to her was her mother, which was true, it was me. You then moved over to me and told me about the new business venture which I was starting and that it would really take off. (I had just opened a shop and it has taken off.) You mentioned my daughter's baby again and said that she would be just like her, in fact, she's her double.

You said the man had passed away with emphysema which had started when he was in the war. In fact, he'd spent two days in the sea at Dunkirk and this eventually caused him problems later on. This was all correct. You then said that he was Irish and that he had ginger hair, again correct. I just wanted to thank you for the help you gave to us that evening.'
Pam, Doncaster.

After the charity meeting a number of other organisations approached me for bookings. Work then just started to snowball. Each day I would receive half a dozen or so letters asking if I could take a meeting, or for some private sittings. The interest in the work I was doing, was quite phenomenal to say the least. During that first year we raised thousands of pounds for various charities, so not only were they helped, but also the people who attended the meetings, they were helped by the comfort and evidence delivered to them from their loved ones in spirit.

My college work was soon beginning to suffer quite badly as I was concentrating more and more on my spiritual development. I knew that I had to draw the line somewhere and so I decided to dramatically cut down on the meetings and concentrate on my course work and finding a part time job to help see me through college. I'd had to give up my job at the night club because of starting the course and the small grant that I'd received had nearly run out.

I asked the spirit world if they could help me as this was a need and much to my surprise Naiomi was able to tell me that I should go to a local Job Centre where I would find the ideal part time job.

The following morning I decided to take the spirit world's advice and go to the Job Centre. As I scanned the various vacancy boards one particular job advert caught my eye. It was for a Senior Night Care Officer in a home for elderly people. The job was perfect as it was for week end work. I made a note of the number and asked the clerk at reception for further details. She gave the home a call and asked me if I could go straight away for an interview. I agreed, even though I felt a little under dressed.

When I arrived at Wyndthorpe Hall I was asked to complete an application form. The lady in the office took the form from me and told me that they would be in touch. I must admit that I did feel rather disappointed travelling all of that way and then not getting an interview. On the way home Naiomi whispered to me,

'Just wait ten days,' she said.
A few days had passed and I was still trying to work out my finances. I had only a very small grant and anyone who's been a student will know that the grants

are no where near enough to be able to survive on.

Exactly ten days after calling at Wyndthorpe Hall I received a letter asking me to get in contact with them. I gave them a call and the lady at the other end of the phone explained that they had been checking references before getting in touch with me and she was very apologetic for it taking time.

'Now, can you start this Friday?' she said.

'Yes,' I gasped, 'what time do you want me to be there?'

The lady suggested that I should arrive for nine thirty so that the day staff would have the chance to give me a quick induction. Naiomi had been right yet again.

Wyndthorpe Hall was a very large grand stately home which had been refurbished to make it suitable for elderly people. The foyer was massive with ornate decorations. It had one of those thick pile velvety type carpets. Suspended some forty feet in the air was a huge brass chandelier. It must have been at least a metre and a half in span. About another twenty feet above that there was a very large glass dome which housed the brass chain mountings that held the chandelier in place.

I'd seen some brass light fittings in my time but this really did take the biscuit.

The rest of the hall was a mixture of old and new tastefully decorated to make the residents feel as comfortable as possible. I was to work regularly on nights with Christine, a nurse. We hit it off straight away and so I knew I was going to enjoy working there.

As the weeks went by Chris and I were able to get better acquainted. After the manual jobs of cleaning the rooms and helping the residents to bed we would often sit in the foyer and have our supper whilst chatting in general. Chris knew that I was a medium because some of her friends had seen me work. She told me that Wyndthorpe had a resident ghost and asked if

I could find anything out about it.

'If they come to talk to me, I can.' I replied.

One evening, in fact it was about two thirty in the morning. Chris has just asked me if I wanted a drink. 'Tea please Chris.' I shouted as she was walking into the kitchen. I took up my usual seat in the foyer right under the chandelier. I could hear Chris washing the cups in the sink when all of a sudden there was an almighty bang. I ran up the stairs as fast as I could whilst doing so my pager started bleeping. It showed a call coming from bedroom three. I rushed down the corridor and into room three.

It suddenly dawned on me that bedroom three was an empty room. I stood in the doorway for a few moments and noticed that the emergency button was underneath the bed. 'Everything all right Paul ?' I heard Chris shout. Before I had chance to answer, my pager started bleeping again. It was bedroom three. There was only me in the room and yet the button had definitely been pushed.

Chris came rushing up the stairs, down the corridor and into the room. I looked at her in a state of numbness. 'I guess it's your ghost Chris.' I said. Just to be on the safe side we decided to check on each resident as well as the doors, windows and outside of the building. There was no sign of anything. Chris and I just looked at each other, shrugged and went back to the foyer to have our supper.

About twenty minutes later, Chris was just reading a magazine when I asked her if she could feel a draft. She nodded in agreement. 'It seems to be coming down from the ceiling.' I said, starting to look up as I did so. To my utter astonishment this large chandelier was swaying from side to side. We both knew that there was no way any of the residents could have possibly moved it. You would have needed a scaffolding platform to do so. I decided to send a thought to Naiomi.

Within a matter of seconds I felt her calming influence. She was able to tell me that the spirit of a lady who'd been murdered in the hall some two hundred years previous was trying to make her presence felt. 'She was succeeding,' I thought. Naiomi went on to say that the lady had been a maid to the Lord of the Manor. It had been her job to polish the chandelier and brasses. I relayed this to Chris and she confirmed that there had been a story about one of the maids being murdered by a stable hand.

Strangely enough, when the hall was being gutted there was a report about some human bones being found under the floor boards where the cellar had been. We were both intrigued by what Naiomi had told us however, there was more. 'There is a problem with the lift, it must be repaired to avoid danger. The lady has also come to warn you of this.' I told Chris what Naiomi had added. 'We must tell the day staff in the morning,' she said, with a concerned look about her.

The day staff were aware of what I did as a medium so when Chris told them about the lift they said they would get the engineer to take a look at it. On returning to work that evening Sheila, one of the day assistants, told me that the lift had collapsed just after Chris and I had left. She said there were four people in it and it took the fire brigade two hours to get them out. Apparently the chief officer said that he couldn't believe that no one had been injured as the lift had been literally hanging on by a thread. Sheila patted me on the back, 'Keep up the good work Paul,' she said.

This wasn't the first time that the spirit world had warned of impending danger. I was introduced to a lady called Lynn who'd apparently been experiencing weird feelings whilst at home alone and she was sure that she'd heard a baby crying, even though the house was empty. I was asked if I would take a look. Lynn lived in a fairly modern semi detached house.

I walked around outside just to see what I could feel and then went in, upstairs and straight to the spare room at the front of the house. As I walked into the room I could hear the sound of a baby, not crying but gurgling happily. As I looked at the spare bed I could just make out the outline of the small child and I immediately noticed something white around its neck. At the same time I could smell gas. I asked Naiomi for some assistance.

She told me that a few years earlier the previous occupant of the house had lost a small baby which had got caught up in his bed clothes and choked. I asked her why I could smell gas. After a short pause she said that the gas heater on the landing was leaking badly and I was to tell Lynn to get it checked immediately.

I relayed this to Lynn and she phoned the gas board immediately. Within fifteen minutes an engineer arrived. He took a look at the heater and announced that it was very badly fractured, his words were in fact, 'This is a death trap, I'll have to cut off your gas and take it straight out.'

I was a little concerned about the baby so I decided to send a thought out to the spirit world again. Almost immediately, I became aware of an elderly lady. She appeared to be cuddling the baby and smiling. I gave a sigh of relief knowing that there was someone there to care for him.

A few days later a very grateful and surprised Lynn contacted me again. She'd discovered from her neighbour that a single mother had lived in the house before her. It had been empty for two years afterwards because the lady's three month old baby had accidentally got tangled in his bed clothes and choked to death. No body had wanted to live in the house because of this. Lynn said that the baby used to sleep in the front bedroom!

In these cases the spirit world helped by warning of danger. They often work behind the scenes engineering situations and lending a helping hand. In a way I suppose, like guardian angels. Haven't you ever wondered where that gut feeling or reaction was coming from? Well I know I have and during my development I discovered it was Naiomi's way of trying to get through to me before I was able to hear her thoughts clearly.

The spirit world not only help with avoiding the not so nice things, they also guide and advise on the positive situations in our lives helping wherever possible. Our loved ones often help us when they're in the body, so there would be no reason for them not to give assistance from the other side. Providing of course they were able to be of help even if only to lend an ear.

I've discovered, over time that when we pass over we remain the same person. We have the same sense of humour, the same temperament. Everything in our personality stays how it was, with the exception of course of any trauma involved in our passing. In traumatic situations we are guided to come to terms with whatever has taken place. I suppose in a way it's a kind of counselling similar to that which we receive here if we need it.

Some difficult situations may require the experience of a wiser spirit person. With their knowledge and experience of many years of watching our world continually evolve they are often able to give sound advice. This doesn't mean that they have all of the answers though, but what it does mean, is that with their experience they are able to make more sounder judgments. As you'll see with this next story.

It was the last term of college. The two years had just seemed to fly by. The last placement for me was at a residential home for people with physical difficulties. The majority of the residents were quite a bit older than myself and from talking to them I soon realized that there was a lot to be learned.

I had to complete a case study on a resident and I must admit I was a little stuck for choice as most of them had exceptional life stories to tell. There was one young chap there who was the same age as myself and so I thought it would be nice if he agreed, for me to use his experiences as the case study, that way I would be able to compare views, ideas and goals.

Daz, as he is known, went on to tell me his life story. He was born with the umbilical cord around his neck and for a short period of time, he actually passed over. He was soon revived and a few weeks afterwards the Doctors discovered that the lack of oxygen to his brain had caused damage which resulted in him having cerebral palsy. He was subsequently given up for adoption. Quite a chunk of his life was spent in care.

When he was first placed in care he was looked after by two ladies who have since become life long friends and are considered by Daz, to be his family. Phyllis Bowmer and her sister Marion, are very close to him indeed.

As he grew up, Daz went to a special school in Huddersfield which was for young people with physical difficulties. At the same time, he was fostered by a couple who also had three daughters of their own. When he was not at school he would either be staying with Phyllis, or Bowmer as he affectionately calls her, or his foster parents.

When Daz turned eighteen it was time for him to leave school. He was a little too heavy for his foster parents and Phyllis and Marion to manage so he found a place at the home in Doncaster. Daz told me about the dreams he'd often had of having his own place and being able to have pets, rather than being in a home and having to rely on staff for assistance when there were thirty other people needing attention.

Some of the more mobile residents were able to get their own bungalows from the council and whenever this happened I could tell that Daz wished it was he who was moving out.

One day I was going around saying my usual goodbyes to the residents when I came across Daz sitting alone in his room crying. I asked him what was wrong. At the same time I'd noticed that he had some scratches on his hands and face. 'I'm sick of this place,' he said, 'I'd give anything to get out of here.'

'How did you get those cuts, Daz?' I asked.

'My chair tipped over into the rose bushes and I was caught on the thorns. As I tried to move I cut myself even more.'

As it transpired Daz had just literally wanted to curl up and die in the rose bushes. Some things have gotten to me at times but I can honestly say nothing as great as this ever had. With this in mind I called upon the spirit world yet again for some help.

At that time I seemed to get no response. Usually Naiomi would come and talk to me and yet when I needed her most to help someone she wasn't there. 'Don't worry Daz,' I said, 'it will all work out, I promise.'

That evening when I got home I decided to have a talk with the spirit world again. To be honest I was a little bit annoyed because they hadn't responded when there was an urgent need. This time though, Naiomi was there in an instant. I asked her what had happened that afternoon and she explained that there were one or two things that needed to be sorted out before she could respond to my request. She told me that I was to have complete trust and that things would start coming together.

I went into work early the following day to see how Daz was feeling. Just as I got to his room I could hear another one of the residents telling him that he'd got a council bungalow and he would be moving out soon. As I peered round the door I could sense that Daz was starting to feel even more down in himself. When the other resident had gone I nipped in to see him.

'Why don't you put your name on the council waiting list?' I asked. He told me that he did not have anyone who was able to look after him. I felt a prod in my back and at the same time, Naiomi whispered to me,

'You can do it,' she said. 'We'll help you,'

Without a second thought I told Daz that I would help to look after him. His eyes lit up as he asked if we could go to the council offices there and then.

'Why not,' I replied. So off we went to town.

By the time we'd arrived at the council offices there was quite a long queue. After about two and a half hours of waiting it was our turn. I explained the situation to the lady behind the counter and very reluctantly she handed me a form to fill in and arranged an appointment for us to see a housing officer. I filled the form in whilst we were in the office and handed it back to the lady.

The following day Daz received a telephone call from the housing department. He was told that he could go on the waiting list but it would be at least an eight year wait. They also said that there would be no need for him to attend the appointment as he had been put straight on to the list.

In one way Daz was pleased but in many others he was very disappointed. To him there was the prospect of at least another eight years in the home.

A week or so had passed and still Daz seemed down, 'Surely there must be something that I could do?' I thought. Then an idea came to mind. I decided to take Daz to town for lunch and then on to the cinema. It was the least I could do and I knew it would get him out of the home even if it was for only a few hours.

'Get your coat on,' I said, 'we're off out.' Daz looked at me in surprise.

Before lunch, Daz suggested that I book a taxi for when the film had ended so that we wouldn't have to wait too long afterwards. I popped into a phone box in the market place and just as I was about to dial the number, I felt Naiomi's presence, 'Over there,' she said, guiding my thoughts to the opposite side of the road.

I was drawn towards a large notice in an empty shop window it read, 'houses and flats for sale and rent,' giving an address and telephone number of an estate agent. I quickly replaced the receiver and dialled the number. A nice lady at the other end of the phone said that there were quite a number of houses and flats to rent. I quickly explained the circumstances after which she asked me to hold the line.

'Hello sir,' she said, 'We have just one ground floor flat which is to the North of the town you can take a look if...' before she had the chance to finish I asked if we could call and collect the keys,

'Of course sir,' she replied.

I raced out of the phone box took hold of Daz's wheelchair and started to walk very quickly. I told him that the cinema was cancelled. He looked at me sadly. I explained that we were going to take a look at a flat instead. He soon cheered up.

After getting the keys we made our way to where the flat was. It took us some time to find the street. From the outside it didn't look too bad however inside was a different matter. It was very sparse and cold. The decor was really poor and the whole placed looked as if it could do with being gutted.

'Not to worry,' I said, somewhat bravely, 'we can soon fix this place up. What do you think then?' I looked at Daz.
'It'll do me,' he said. By this time he was grinning from ear to ear.
We went back to the estate agents offices and told them that we would take the place. After a few formalities and form filling the lady handed me the keys and a rent book.

'Here you are sir,' she said with a smile.
'Thank you.' I nodded. 'Well Daz,' I said, 'it's up to you when you want to move in.' He never answered straight away. I think it was because he couldn't believe what was happening and there was no doubt that he was wondering if he was going to be let down again.

During the next few days Daz soon perked up and started to get into the spirit of things, so we started to organize the moving arrangements. His foster parents were in the salvation army and so they helped us with furniture beds and carpets. His social worker got him a leaving care grant which helped to buy all of the small essentials and pay for some decorating.

Taking on this kind of responsibility made me realize that I would certainly have my work cut out. I hadn't, to be honest, really thought deeply about what I was doing. One thing's for certain though, I knew the spirit world were quite sure it was the right thing.

Both Daz's and my friends helped out in many different ways. Particularly during our settling in period. As time went on we were able to get Daz's disability benefits sorted out. He was even eligible for some money from a charity to help pay for extra care and so we were able to pay people to help out.

A few weeks after moving in we discovered that an old friend of mine, Pauline, who used to be in the circle, lived just around the corner from us. It made things even better to know that there was someone nearby who we knew. One afternoon she called in on us carrying a small box under her arm.

'I've got you a present Daz,' she said and as she opened the box. A small black and white puppy popped its head out of the top.

'Ah,' said Daz, as Pauline put the puppy on his Knee. 'I think I'll call her Gyp,' he added.

'Gyp?' I replied. Daz nodded. Pauline and I just looked at each other. Gyp was, or rather still is a Jack Russell terrier, or should that be terror? As we were soon to find out.

It was just a few days before Christmas and I'd been out to buy some decorations for the tree. As a treat for Daz I'd bought some of those chocolate Santa Claus and snowmen. The tree looked really nice in the middle of the floor with all the tinsel, ornaments, fairy lights and chocolates. I was just admiring my workmanship with Daz when the phone rang. It turned out to be an old friend who I'd not heard from for quite some time. I was happily chatting when I heard Daz shout.

As I was turning round I froze in my tracks. To my utter astonishment the Christmas tree was rocking from side to side. Now I'd heard of physical phenomena but this was unbelievable. I made an excuse to end the phone call and stared in amazement at the tree. By this time it was really swaying and the lights were beginning to send me dizzy. All of a sudden it fell over. There was a loud yelp and out from under the tree came Gyp looking somewhat upset. Daz and I just rolled about laughing. There we were thinking we were about to see a spirit person materialise before our eyes holding this tree, when all of the time it was Gyp.

As we later found out she'd discovered the taste of chocolate and obviously liked it, so much so, that she decided she would have some more. She'd half eaten all but one of the chocolates. It was so funny that I hadn't the heart to scold her. I knew then that I would have to keep my eye on her, to make sure she wouldn't be getting into any more mischief.

Life for Daz was getting better and better. I noticed a dramatic change in the way he was feeling and I knew he couldn't believe his luck. He'd got his own place, his own staff, as he often joked and a pet dog, all with the help of the spirit world. Together we were able to bring some happiness into Daz's life, happiness which has remained there.

This is of course what it's all about. Not to bring wealth or tell fortunes as many people still believe but to bring a glimmer of, well not just hope but the truth that death is not the end, it's only the beginning of a great adventure and whilst in this world we can seek the guidance and help of the spirit people even if it's only to show our love and thanks to them for the many aspects of our lives, that they are constantly involved in.

They will help us if we are willing to meet them half way by helping ourselves. It's the same principal in both worlds. It's very much a case of 'Seek and you shall find.' We sought the help of the spirit people and we found the right way to go about things, turning the negative into positive with some pretty remarkable results.

Chapter 4

My eyes started to flicker as the train rocked from side to side. I'd had a good nights' sleep so there was no reason for me to feel tired - yet this feeling of drowsiness came all over me, you know, the kind of feeling you get as a child, just as you are going to sleep, that feeling of peace and security.

We were on our way to Hastings. I'd been invited, to take part in a mind body and spirit festival which was being held at the White Rock Theatre. The organisers had been given my name by some people who'd been to one of the meetings and they wanted me to give some lectures and demonstrations. Irene, the lady who'd organized the fairway hotel meeting had since become a good friend of ours and we'd asked her if she wanted to come along. She jumped at the chance.

Both Daz and Irene, looked at me very strangely, 'What's the matter Paul?' asked Irene,

'I'm just feeling very, very....' there was a sudden jerk as if I was being yanked from my seat. Almost instantly, I could see both Irene, Daz and myself all sitting on the train. It was like a birds' eye view of everything. I seemed to start floating upwardly out of my seat and towards the clouds. As I looked down I could see the train disappearing beneath me. The feeling I had was very similar to the one which you have when you've been given a pre-med just before an operation. It's that feeling of great tiredness. You want to sleep but find it very difficult and then you start to become restless.

In my thoughts I asked Naiomi for help,

'Don't worry,' she said rather casually, 'this has been planned for sometime.'

At first I thought my time had arrived, 'I haven't even got things tied up yet,' I said , quite concerned by this time.

'You're not coming here to stay,' Naiomi said adding, 'You asked if you could meet your people.'
'That was months ago,' I replied.
'Well,' said Naiomi, 'The time for this has arrived. Now have...'

Before she had the chance to finish another voice interrupted the conversation,

'Paul, Paul.'

I knew straight away who it was. As I looked ahead of me I could see the faint outline of a person with a dog standing by their side.

'Dad,' I said, 'it is you. I've missed you so much.' I said as I raced towards him. 'I'm sorry for all of the trouble I caused you. Can you forgive me?'

'Oh Paul, he said, 'there's no rush, slow down. There's nothing to forgive you for. Everyone has arguments and disagreements. It's part of life.' Dad said sympathetically.

'I just feel so responsible,' I said.

In the mean time the dog came to sit by my side. It was Jackie, my dad's dog. I didn't know her because she'd passed over before I was born. She still had her beautiful black coat though, the one I'd seen in pictures of her. I crouched down and patted her on the back. She jumped up to give my face a lick. Her tail was wagging furiously.

'Are you happy Dad?' I asked.

'Much happier than I was,' he replied. 'It took me some time to understand what went wrong. I was helped by my Gran, when I got over here and then I met Paul.'

'How is he Dad?' I asked.

'At the beginning he told me he was angry. If the lights had of been on red he said he might have been in with a chance. As time has passed he's gradually come to terms with everything. He's with his Grandad.'

I told you about Paul's accident earlier. One thing that I didn't say was that apparently there were some traffic lights and a bridge just before the bend where Paul was killed. A number of people had said that if the traffic lights had been on red there would have been no car and it was possible that Paul may have survived.

'Oh, Dad,' I added. 'What about Nan. Look what happened to her.'

'She didn't feel anything Paul. I know she could see what was going to happen but you must believe me, it was all so quick. She's sometimes with your Grandad.'
'Sometimes?' I queried.
'Well they still don't get on,' he added. 'Dad will see her but he doesn't want her around him all of the time.'

I laughed. 'They never change do they?'

I couldn't believe what was happening. Was I dreaming or was it for real? There was no reason for me to suddenly just 'fall asleep' and then dream this.
'It's for real,' Dad said. 'I can see what you're thinking as clearly as you can see me,' he added.

There were so many things I wanted to say and ask that my mind had gone completely blank. I was just beginning to get used to the idea when my eyes started to feel heavy again and I felt Naiomi gently touched my

65

arm.

'It's time to go,' she said.
'No..., no not yet,' I cried.

There was a sudden jolt and I found myself sitting back in the train carriage. In the distance I could just make out Dad's voice.

'Bye son, bye.' I stared somewhat dazed, at Irene.

'How long have I been gone?' I asked.
'You haven't been anywhere,' she said. 'You drifted off a couple of minutes ago.'

'A couple of minutes?' I thought. Naiomi leant towards me.

'Now you're not sure, are you?'
'Well..' I fumbled.
'Just remember how he looked,' she added.

It dawned on me a few seconds later, what she'd meant. Dad had somehow looked different. He seemed to look younger without the worry and age lines. Of course I realized that he would look younger simply because he didn't have a physical body. Now if I'd have been dreaming, he would of looked like he did when he was in the body. I started to feel elated inside. I'd really been to visit Dad.

All of this time spent searching going to church hoping for a message, joining the circle and hoping that he would make contact, constantly asking the spirit world if I could see him just one more time. They finally managed to make it possible. I couldn't thank Naiomi enough. She went on to tell me something very interesting.

'If you had gotten what you wanted in the beginning,' she said, 'would you have followed the road you have taken today?'

I paused for a moment. She went on.

'We know that you may have done so for a short time but we had to make sure that you followed your life plan according to the way which was right for you.'

So the spirit world had all of this planned. Some medium I was. I had no idea whatsoever. Naiomi was right though I think I would have followed this path just for a short time and then got on with my life as I believed it should be.

The spirit people obviously felt that I would be an asset to their cause and so they ensured that I followed the way which they knew was the right one.

I told Daz and Irene what had happened, they looked at me disbelievingly.

'Don't you believe me,' I snapped.

It wasn't that they didn't believe me Irene explained, it was because they were both as amazed as I was and just as stuck for words. It certainly made our journey to Hastings a lot better, because we had plenty to talk about. It also helped to take my mind off the work that I had ahead of me.

We got to Hastings in what seemed to be no time at all. The White Rock Theatre was a beautiful place. It was a chalky white coloured building, (probably where they got the name from,) overlooking the sea right near to a kind of harbour. When we got inside we were shown around the venue and introduced to some of the people who had stalls there.

There were craft stalls, crystal stalls, books, tapes, people selling spa's for the bath. You name it they were all there.

The people just flocked in to the festival and it was constantly busy. The whole place was alive with the sound of voices and music.

The lectures and demonstrations I did seemed to go down very well indeed. However one particular question kept on popping up during lectures. It was about the fact that I was only twenty one. People were surprised that I was a medium at such a young age.

I think a lot of the reason was because it was at that time that Doris Stokes, Doris Collins and Gordon Higginson, were all frequently appearing in the public eye. So perhaps the people had this idea that a medium must need to be of a more mature age.

Well I always say that you either are a medium or not. Irrespective of age, creed, colour, sex or status. Being mature is of course very important in mediumship, however it doesn't necessarily come with age. It can, more often than not, come with experience and I certainly felt that I'd had enough of that to help me understand at least a little of life.

Funnily enough after they had seen me demonstrate they didn't appear to think any more of it. It was quite strange really that some of them were apprehensive because of my age. It's almost as if they'd made up their minds before giving me a fair crack of the whip. It only goes to show how wrong we all can be at times, as often we can be judgmental without giving fair thought to the situation only realising later that we were wrong and no doubt feeling quite remorseful.

One time Naiomi taught me a very valuable lesson about this.

I had been judgmental about a situation concerning a friend. After having it pointed out to me by the spirit world, with great remorse I apologised to both them and the friend, only realising I was wrong, when my thoughts had been spoken back to me. For quite a while afterwards I felt somewhat ashamed of myself and it was obvious to me that the spirit world knew about this. One evening Naiomi came to me.

'We are by no means perfect,' she told me.

'I know, but.' she interrupted.

'You have learned to recognise your mistakes,' she said, adding, 'as long as you do, you can try to make sure that they do not happen again.'

I felt a little better for what she'd said and since then I have tried to put it into practice, not always succeeding though.

Going back to talking about Doris Stokes, a few days after returning from Hastings, a friend telephoned me to say that Doris was appearing at Sheffield City Hall. Hazel told me that they had bought some tickets and two of the people who were supposed to be going had given them back word. Without any hesitation, I asked if I could have them.

'We're all going in a minibus,' said Hazel.

'That's no problem, I replied.

As it turned out Daz had arranged to stay with friends in Huddersfield. He was a little disappointed but we both agreed that we would go to see her the next time she was in Sheffield, or any where else nearby. I decided to ask Paul's mother if she wanted to go along. I hadn't seen her for quite some time and so it was an ideal opportunity to catch up on things. She'd already seen Doris when she appeared in Lincoln and as I suspected she didn't want to miss out on seeing her again.

Every time I'd wanted to go along to an evening with Doris Stokes all of the tickets had usually sold out. Doris sold tickets like hot cakes, faster than many of the top pop groups and artistes. This was my first real opportunity to see her and there was no way I was going to miss it. I'd once seen her on television and read about her in the *Psychic News*, but most of what I knew had come from other people who'd been fortunate enough to get tickets for her meetings.

Over two and a half thousand people packed in to Sheffield City Hall. We were sitting right up in the Gods and believe me, it felt like it!

Our seats were in the area that offered a restricted view, however with a little strategic positioning we were able to see the centre of the stage.

Doris soon stepped out into the continuous sound of applause. Even when she took her seat the clapping didn't stop. She looked very much the person, we'd all heard about with a quaint positively friendly grandmotherly approach.

The sound system in the city hall was not very good at all, added to this was the fact that Doris was still recovering from a stroke. It did make it difficult at times, for us to hear what she was saying.

Doris's warmth and sense of humour did however shine through. The messages she gave were marvellous and her delivery was second to none. I must say that it was well worth waiting all of that time just to see her.

I have never forgotten that evening. I can still picture myself just sitting there being a part of all of that warmth and feeling. Sadly, Daz never did get to see Doris, for she passed over in May 1987. I'm quite sure that in her own way she is still delivering that remarkable warmth and love to us all.

I have heard many comments about Doris since she passed over. Much to my, dismay a lot of them have been negative and in some cases down right bitchy, if you pardon the expression.

A lot of these came from people who claimed to be spiritual. I often wonder why they never took the time to perhaps write and tell Doris whilst she was here, what they thought and how they felt. Maybe deep down they realised the truth and perhaps they couldn't face it.

Although I never personally knew Doris, even though like many others I felt I did, I have come to realize through my own work exactly what she has done for many thousands of people.

She gave a lot often for very little in return and to my mind she deserves the respect she earned. She updated spiritualism so much so, that there became a new stronger element of membership.

I shall always speak of her with the highest regard as I do, some of the other great mediums like Doris Collins, Gordon Higginson, Albert Best and many others for that matter.

These people have helped pave the way for all of us, not just mediums or spiritualists, but everyone who has had that need of comfort and knowledge, that need which comes from the heart, the need to talk with our loved ones again and discover the truth of life eternal beyond this world.

Chapter 5

'Right Mr Norton I want you to read that registration number on the red car over there,' said the driving examiner.

I'd been taking lessons for some time now and I got that sick of waiting for my instructor to let me know when he felt I was ready for my test, that I decided to go ahead and book it myself.

With all of the work I had coming in and not being able to get Daz on to public transport we decided that we needed something of our own. Daz suggested that I take driving lessons and if I passed my test we would be able get a car by using his mobility allowance. To be honest although it was much needed I'd never really given it much thought, that was until Daz suggested it. I agreed knowing that it would be the best thing.

I'd arranged for Daz to stay with Sam, Yvonne and Janet, some friends of ours. Sam often read the tarot cards and he and Janet, who is a very good medium, would often go to Thoresby market in Nottinghamshire and literally set up a stall and do sittings. Daz and I used to make jokes about it.
Yvonne, Sam's wife, would gladly welcome people into the house. She wasn't really a spiritualist but she would often listen to our many conversations and debates about spiritualism.

As I set off for my last lesson they all wished me luck. My driving instructor wasn't impressed with the fact that I'd arranged my test date, he still thought I was no where near ready. On the way to the test centre, I asked Naiomi for help.

'Just watch that stick,' she said, whilst guiding my thoughts towards the gear stick, 'and you'll be fine, I promise, you will pass.'

On previous occasions I'd found the gear stick to be a little awkward. My instructor had promised to get it seen to but he never did. Each time I put the car into third gear, it would slip out and then you'd hear a grinding sound and if I wasn't careful, the car would just slow down to a halt.

So here I was, just beginning my test. I read the registration number without any problems and got into my car. The examiner was a very large stern looking fellow, I think they're all like that, may be not large, but certainly stern looking. He asked me to start the car and follow the directions that he was going to give me. We first went to a quiet area of the town, where I had to do an emergency stop. We then went on, to do a three point turn, reversing round a corner and then a hill start.

By this time I was beginning to enjoy myself and I noticed that the examiner was looking much happier as well. On the way back to the test centre I was just moving into third gear, when the gear stick slipped straight back out. My heart stood still for a split second, as I fought with the gear leaver.

'Take your time Paul,' I heard Naiomi whisper.

The car had slowed down quite a lot by now and there was a build up of traffic behind us. I looked over to the examiner, smiled rather apologetically, took a deep breath, put the car into gear and moved off. Despite feeling somewhat flustered I breathed a sigh of relief.

When we got back to the test centre the examiner asked me to park the car and he then went on to ask me some questions about driving. I might have driven the car alright, but when it came to the questions, my mind went blank. I quickly asked for some assistance from the spirit world.

To my surprise the examiner started telling me the answers, with a quick, 'You knew that, didn't you?' after each one.

I just couldn't believe my luck. I'd heard all these things about how strict the examiners were and that they very rarely spoke, unless it was to give direction and here I was getting all of the answers. I knew at that point the outcome of my test.

'Mr Norton,' said the examiner in that unmistakable stern tone, ' I'm pleased to tell you that you've passed your driving proficiency test.'

My thoughts went straight to the spirit world. 'Thank you so much,' I said silently. I couldn't wait to get back to tell the others. On the way home I couldn't resist smirking. My driving instructor just carried on watching the road ahead he didn't seem the least bit interested that I'd passed.

When I got back I could see Janet looking out of the window. I quickly tried to fake a solemn expression and walked unenthusiastically into the house.

'Well,' said Janet, 'You've done it haven't you?' I couldn't bare it any longer and a broad grin came across my face.

'Yes, I've passed,' I said, jumping in the air. Daz burst into tears of joy and Sam shook my hand.

'You'll be needing this,' said Yvonne, whilst passing me a much appreciated cup of tea.

'I saw it in the cards,' said Sam.

'Well why didn't you tell me then?' I asked.

'I wasn't sure it was right,' he said with a chuckle. Old Sam, as we called him used to make us laugh. He would sit there in his chair making signs with his hands repeating the words, 'You come and I give, you come and I give.' He would then give you a reading, during which he would start talking about the spirit world and give you a message from whoever was there.

Afterwards, he would deny that there was a spirit world.

'I don't mess with that tinky tonk.' He would say.

Many a time Daz and I would roll in fits of laughter.

Janet was no better. She used to get all of us laughing, so much so, that tears would roll down our cheeks. The night before my driving test she told us about the time that Sam had taken her on a driving lesson just before her test.

'He told me to go across the roundabout, so I did,' she said innocently.

'Yes,' added Sam. 'But I didn't mean you should drive straight over the thing.'

We were in hysterics poor old Janet and Sam had got stuck on the verge of this roundabout with the car tilted over to one side. We could just picture Sam shouting the words.

'Get out, get out, you're not driving any more,' whilst turning crimson with anger. It didn't end there though at the end of Janet's test her examiner asked her what she would not do on a motorway. Before she answered she looked at her cigarettes longingly.

'Well I wouldn't light up a cigarette,' she said.

'Come come Mrs Vaughan,' came his reply. 'Surely you can wait five more minutes?'

Once Janet and Sam got together that was it you wouldn't have a dry eye for ages.

Janet was that much of a tonic that Sam suggested that she come along to Doncaster Civic Theatre with me to chair a meeting we had booked. What with my driving test and getting settled into flat and going to see Doris Stokes, I'd clean forgotten about the meeting and it was only a couple of days away. I thought it would be nice, in fact I suggested to Janet that she might like to work along side of me.

'Well, I'm not sure,' she said.
'Go on Janet,' Sam chipped in. 'Show 'em what you're made of.'
'Well, if you're sure Paul.'
'I'm certain,' I said. 'So that settles it.'

The evening soon arrived. Janet and Sam arranged to pick us up. They arrived very early so we decided to go along to the theatre and get everything set up. We'd bought some artificial flowers for a centre piece and some fresh ones to line the stage with. Janet had even bought both of us a white carnation, to wear on stage. After setting up, we went to the dressing rooms to have a cigarette and cup of tea.

The theatre seated five hundred people and we knew that over half of the tickets had been sold before the evening. I was just explaining this to Janet when one of the theatre staff knocked at the door. He wanted us to test the microphones.

'Have you any idea exactly how many tickets have gone?' I asked.
'At the last count,' he replied, 'this morning, over three hundred and eighty.'

Janet and I looked at each other.
'Well,' I said, 'if you can do it in front of one then what's another four hundred?'
'Who are you trying to convince Paul?' Janet added.

By the time we were about to start both Janet and I were furiously praying for help from the spirit world.

'It's a little late now.' I said whilst we were waiting in the wings.

The introduction announcement was made. Janet gave me a prod and push as we walked out towards the centre of the stage to the thunderous sound of clapping hands. The theatre was packed with people in rows stretching right to the back.

Janet demonstrated first and she did very well. I then followed with equal enthusiasm from the audience.

Another friend of ours, Keith had agreed to pass the microphone around. The messages were going in all different directions so poor old Keith was having to walk backwards, forwards, sideways and the same again.

The evening turned out to be a great success. Afterwards, when the people would let us get through, after inquiring about messages and sittings, we went back to Sam's house and toasted our success with a bottle of wine.

'You both worked well together,' said Sam. 'Why not do some more?'

Both Janet and I agreed and so we decided to make arrangements to meet and organise some more demonstrations.

I got quite a lot of requests for private sittings, from people who'd been at the Civic Theatre. Because I had a few weeks to spare before my next meeting I decided to take some bookings. One family had asked me if I could go to their house. It wasn't normal practice for me to do so, but because they lived quite near by and there were four of them, I agreed. A few days after the sitting, I received some letters from each one of them expressing their gratitude. Here's what they said.

Dear Paul
I did not really know what to expect when I booked the tickets for the Civic Theatre on the evening of your appearance. I do know that I thought you could maybe help.

You see, prior to the show, my eldest brother had passed away quite suddenly and it had been a great shock to us all. You did not really speak to my mother and I individually but you did agree to come for a private sitting at my mother's home.

As I said before, none of us really knew what to expect. I am so glad - we are all so glad - that you did see us privately. We were all nursing our own private griefs and thoughts and I know that you helped each one of us. I won't say that I was cynical, prior to meeting you - in fact I had an open mind.

Some of the things you said were only thoughts in my head, some were not even disclosed to other members of the family. You said that I would receive a bill for £78 which I have, but I was not to worry about it - quite correctly it has been sorted out and I didn't have to pay it.

Naturally you cannot take all our grief away, but you have restored our beliefs and you have certainly made me feel better about many things.

I think you are so lucky to have such a great gift and I hope that you will continue to help people and be a comfort to them in their time of need. I am convinced that our loved ones are always around us and I cannot say how much this thought is of comfort to me. I could go on and on, but I won't. Just one more thing - keep up the good work!
                                Elaine Pearce

Dear Paul,
I would just like to say I was a bit frightened when you came to our house, because I didn't think my brother would have forgiven me. We were once or twice good friends until his last few days before he passed away.

I would like to thank you for reuniting me with my brother and for putting something special into our lives and helping me regain my faith in the life after death.
I'm now not scared of passing over to the other side, thanks to you Paul. Till next time, Dave (aged 15)

Dave's brother had nothing to forgive him for, as he told us, 'The fall outs are part of family life.'

It was so nice to be able to reassure someone who had their whole earthly life ahead of them, giving them the knowledge that life continues beyond this world.

Dear Paul
What can I possibly add to all that my son and daughter have said? Only that I felt a great weight had been lifted from me. I had looked after my son during his long illness and I felt so bitter about his passing, until you talked to us all and passed on messages from him - so obviously him - I recognised his sense of humour.

I know now that some day I will be with him again - in a better place.
Thank you from all of us once again
Mrs M Joyce

Letters like these are the real rewards behind the work of a medium. Sometimes you work so hard, even at odd hours, travelling from place to place feeling somewhat negative at times and yet when you get home, sit down and read through some of things people write, it brings a tremendous sense of satisfaction and positive feeling. Which makes you want to go out and touch upon the lives of as many people as possible allowing the spirit world to pour some light and love onto them.

One lady wrote to me after she'd had a sitting. I met her at Bridlington, and as it transpired, she was from Germany. I was a little worried, because I didn't, and still don't, know the german language. The spirit world however, were able to help in a remarkable way.

Bridlington 1st May
I first saw Paul Norton demonstrating at a meeting in Bridlington, where he gave extremely good evidence of survival to a very good friend of mine. That same night, I arranged to have a private sitting with him.

Paul Norton had never met me before. During this sitting, Paul produced proof of survival in great many details, which left me beyond any doubt: there is not just a life after death and a very well informed one about our problems as such, but also a way of communication through mediums like Paul.

It must have been very difficult for him, as my country of origin is Germany. Many names of relatives and places from my home country were given to me. Here I would just like to mention a few, like; my grandmother, Olga, with full description, my mother, Maria, inclusive detail from her life and items now in my possession, also my uncles, Anton, Johann, Hans and Vogt. Places like Oberammergau, Weil, Weinheim and in particular Gutersloh were named. Gutersloh is a small town in Westphalia, where my Grandmothers' relatives originated from. If he was given a name of place, Paul could not pronounce, he would spell it, relating to me a recognisable german word.

Repeating Paul Norton's own words: if he can give true proof, help and comfort to only one person, his efforts are worth while. I hope he can give this proof to many people.

Ingrid M. Feuchte

Ingrid was a lovely lady. During the sitting she noticed my nervousness and so she tried and succeeded in helping me to relax, so that her loved ones were able to communicate with her. This for me constitutes remarkable evidence not only did I not have prior knowledge about Ingrid, as in the case of all of the sittings I do, but I had no knowledge at all about Germany and German names.

One final letter came from a lady we'd met in London. We'd been invited by Marion Massey, (the lady who discovered and managed the singer Lulu,) to have tea with Michael Endacott of the institute of complimentary medicine and herself. Marion's home was also her office. Her assistant Patrina, was asked to join us. During tea I sensed that there was something emotionally wrong with Patrina. As it turned out she suspected that she possibly had cancer and was naturally very worried whilst awaiting medical results. I tuned in to the spirit world and was able to tell her that she did not have cancer. Here's what she wrote.

Dear Paul and Daz

It was so wonderful meeting you all. Your message Paul came true and I didn't have cancer of the breast. I still have to be checked every six months. You certainly were an inspiration to me.
I wish you well in your career. I know that you will do well. I hope I'll be able to help you.
With lots of love from

Patrina xxxxx
East Barnet, Hertfordshire.

I knew that Patrina was in the clear but all the same to hear the news confirmed was such a relief, both for Patrina and ourselves. She is a lovely lady and she certainly deserves to be helped in any way possible.

Talking about wonderful people in need, I remember one time I had a radio interview.

'Good morning, you're listening to Radio York, this is Kate Kaverner with the mid morning show and the time is just coming up to nine fifty. My special guest this morning will be Paul Norton. Paul is a medium and he'll be doing his thing over the phone. So if you'd like to speak to Paul give us a call on York 641641, that's York 641641 in around about an hours' time.'

I wonder what people thought? 'doing his thing over the phone.' We were on our way to York and this was the announcement we heard on the radio. We were doing a meeting in Scarborough and radio York had got wind of it so they invited me to take part in an interview and phone in. I'd never been on the radio before and so was a little nervous and of course excited.

We arrived at the studio in good time and the reception staff made us very welcome indeed.
'Tea Mr Norton?' inquired the young lady on reception.
'No thank you,' I said. 'Oh, by the way, just call me Paul.'
'Ok Paul,' she said, adding, 'would you care for a sandwich or biscuit.' I was a bit too nervous to eat anything, in fact I was more frightened that I might not have been able to keep it down!

About five minutes before the interview I was taken upstairs to the studio and introduced to Kate Kaverner. She was very bright and bubbly. Kate explained to me the course of the interview and what she intended to do about the phone in.

'Now, do you think you've got that?' she asked.
'Yes, I think so.' Kate showed me where to sit and how to adjust the headset and microphone.

It was very interesting. All of these little gadgets, dials and wires all over the place. I was quite surprised at the set up. Whenever you're listening to the radio you always imagine some cosy little room at the top of a building with a lovely view. Well the studio was quite large not very cosy at all and the only window was the one which looked straight into the producer's room. The thought of having to spend the best part of each day and week stuck in there made me realize how well off I was. At least I could go outside into the garden in the summer and do sittings there if I wanted to.

It was soon time to start. Kate gave me a quick introduction and went on to ask what it was exactly that I did. I explained a bit about the spirit world and how a medium works at which point Kate interrupted.

'But don't you think that these messages are at times somewhat prosaic?' She said, 'Like don't leave the iron on or you'll burn your dress?'

'Prosaic?' what on earth did she mean? I thought. 'Err well no, not really,' I said hastily. She went on,

'Not even a little bit ordinary?' So that's what she meant.

'Well you have to remember that these people who communicate are very ordinary people, no different from you or I. They would only mention relevant facts, thoughts and feelings. If a person was forgetful, say for instance with an iron, their loved ones in spirit would no doubt mention it, along with anything else that they felt was important.'

Kate went on. 'I've seen some of these people in action and I wonder if they plant people in the audience.'

'Well anyone who knows me well enough, will also know that if I have a message for them, I will usually tell them after any meeting. I will never give a message to a person I know, in an audience. Or at least not knowingly or intentionally and I don't believe any other genuine medium would, either.'

Kate went on to tell people about the meeting in Scarborough and that the lines were open for calls. Within seconds, all of these little red lights started flashing in front of me.

'The lines are jammed Paul,' said Kate.

I couldn't believe it. We'd only intended to take three or four calls and now we had a load of people wanting to ask questions, in the hope of a message. Kate's producer suggested that we should take all of the calls, but because of the time factor, it would be better to carry on off air. I didn't mind at all so the producer took me next door into her control room.

One by one, I took each call. Some people were asking about the meeting at Scarborough but most were looking for some sign of hope. One lady came on the line and she sounded very sad indeed.

'I have a gentlemen who's giving me the name Rob, but he's saying Rob and Bob.'

'Yes,' came the lady's reply, 'Rob is my husband and Bob is my son.'

'He's telling me that he passed with cancer, in the stomach.'

'That's true.'

'This must only have been recently, he's showing me five, yes, five weeks ago, is that right?' By this time the lady was crying uncontrollably.

'Yes,' she sobbed.

'He said it was very quick, all over in a week.'

'He was diagnosed on the Monday,' she said, 'and he passed away the following Monday.'

'Well, he says I'm to tell you that he loves you very much indeed and he's got Pa and Sid with him.'

'Pa is his Dad and Sid is mine,' she said.

'I have to tell you that the house is safe. He says you are not to concern yourself, it's quite safe.' With that the contact just faded.

Afterwards the lady explained that her husbands' insurance had run out and she was worried about losing the house because she didn't have enough to pay the mortgage. We discovered some time later, that the lady's husband's insurance company had agreed to pay as he had only missed one premium and this had been due the week he'd fallen ill..

I think that this was one of the best sittings, of the day. There was a genuine need for that lady and her husband, Rob. He communicated very well to let her know that everything was in good hands.

Most of the other people wanted messages about their lives, you know, like fortune telling. In fact many times when people have wanted sittings I have had to ask them whether or not they wanted spirit sittings.

Most of them usually say no, in which case I let them know that I am not the type of person who they really want to see.

People often ask if I feel that I'm letting someone down by turning them away. Well my answer to that is, generally speaking, no. You see, as in the case of Patrina and the lady who telephoned Radio York, the spirit world obviously knew that there was a great need. Fair enough, I was already in Patrina's company, at Marion's house and yet, I had no intentions of working, but, because there was a need and Patrina hadn't asked me for help, the spirit world obviously, as I did, felt duty bound to oblige. It's all right people saying, 'well I am in need.' Usually, but not always, those that are most in need will not ask for help or even mention any problems that they may have.

If I am unable to help them I almost always put them in contact, with someone who I feel can. Pam, the lady who wrote to me about her daughter's message at the Fairway Hotel, has since developed her psychic ability. She reads cards for people. I must say that I along with many others, have found her to be very accurate and helpful. So if people want that sort of help, I give them Pam's office telephone number. Equally, if Pam gets a person, who is desperate for a spirit contact she gives them my telephone number.

It's not just a case of saying sorry and putting the phone down on them leaving them in the lurch. I do try my hardest to be of help. Mind you, when you start to receive calls at two and three in a morning, you don't always find it easy to be helpful!

Chapter 6

'Mr Norton..?' asked the worried sounding voice.
'Yes,' I replied cautiously.
'Mr Paul Norton..?'
'Yes.' Again.
'We're not sure what to do there's loads of people and no more tickets I'm getting loads of calls and people coming in to reception. The papers keep ringing up asking for your number. They're threatening to stop the meeting. I asked my boss and she told me to phone you. It's such a mess.'

'Now calm down,' I said 'Lets start again slowly. First of all who are you?'
'I'm Jill the box office receptionist at the Arts Centre.'
'Right Jill what seems to be the problem?'
'We've sold all of your tickets and people still keep calling in and phoning for more.'
'Ok,' I said, 'lets arrange an extra night.'
'The papers want to talk to you because the Christian outreach group are threatening to stop the meeting, they've..' I interrupted.

'Jill you've lost me.' I said, by now even more confused. 'Now what do the papers want?'
'They want to interview you about the petition.'
'What petition?' I asked.
'The Christian outreach group are trying to ban the meeting. They have a five hundred signature petition, they're taking it to the council.' She said sounding quite concerned.
'Let's get this straight,' I said. 'First of all we've sold out of tickets?'
'Yes,' replied Jill.
'Right then Jill I'll get on to Glenda and arrange an extra evening. Now which paper wants to speak to me?'

'All of them,' she said anxiously.

'Well I'll give them a call this afternoon. Now what's this about a petition?'

Jill went on to explain that a local Christian group had got up a five hundred signature petition and presented it to the council to try and prevent a meeting we had booked, going ahead. She told me that they'd had a lot of press and they'd threatened to join hands around the arts centre to prevent people getting in.

'Well,' I said, 'we'll see about that. Don't worry Jill and thank you for calling, I'll be in touch soon.' Poor old Jill she was being harassed from all angles and I'd had no idea until she'd telephoned me.

Janet Vaughan and I had decided to book a number of meetings. Rotherham Arts centre was one of them. It had proved so popular in the past that I'd been appearing there nearly every other month and this was to be the sixth time within a year. The tickets had already gone and there were still two weeks to go. Apparently hundreds more people wanted to come along.

Because of the popularity of previous meetings and the good press we'd received a local Christian outreach group had taken it upon themselves to picket council meetings to try and get mediums, in particular myself, banned.

In the past I'd been able to tolerate the misgivings of such groups but this time I was furious. I spoke to a local reporter who wanted my reaction on the latest events. I made it very clear to him that I intended to stand my ground and if need be I would put up a good fight, for our basic right of freedom.

In the mean time I wrote some very strong letters to the particular council committee who was dealing with, what by now had turned out to be more of an inquisition. The council initially agreed that the dates already booked could go ahead and any future bookings would have to wait until the outcome of the council's findings.

Much to my annoyance and adding to the already created aggravation, a local spiritualist church and a representative of the Spiritualists' National Union had each sent letters to the council and local newspapers protesting at the bigotry of this Christian group. Their letters however seemed to stir up more problems and at that point, although grateful for the thought, I could have really done without them.

It made me laugh in a way because since I'd been taking public meetings I'd experienced more animosity from spiritualist quarters than I had from anywhere else. Around some of churches they were saying hurtful and nasty things and implying that I was making out to be too good for them, yet I'd never said so.

Fortunately by the time the day of the meeting arrived a lot of the aggravation had died down. As planned we booked the centre for another night so that everyone who wanted to come along could do so.

When Janet and I arrived at the arts centre, there was a steady stream of people going in to the building. As we got to the front doors we were suddenly faced with about forty odd people shouting at us.

'Ban the devil worshippers, evil witches, false spirits....,' whilst waiving placards and thrusting leaflets about. Janet and I just looked at each other and continued through to the second lot of doors.

Just in the foyer, much to our annoyance and shock, there were these two elderly ladies being accosted by the so called 'Christians'.

'Christian,' I shouted, 'you don't know the meaning of the word. Now let these two ladies through at once.' I think the picketers were surprised with my reaction. I had no option though, these ladies were getting upset.

'Oh thank you Paul,' they both said, adding, 'it is Paul Norton isn't it?' I nodded.

'It is and don't you mention it. If you have any more problems will you let one of the security guards know?'

'Oh yes,' they both replied, 'we will.'

I don't know how many other people had been set upon but during the meeting I apologised for any upset that had been caused.

Although a little late, we finally managed to get started. Janet took the first half of the meeting and she worked very well indeed giving quite a lot of messages out. All of this excitement over the weeks had obviously got her adrenalin flowing just as much as it had mine.

During my demonstration, a young girl of fifteen made contact with her sister.

'She says it's Carol.' I said.

'Yes cried her sister, 'that's my name.'

'She's taking me to Herring, Herring Road? by the shops she says, we hit a lamp post, I wasn't supposed to be in the car.'

'It was by the shops on Herringthorpe Road and they did hit a lamp post. She'd only gone to the chip shop and was offered a lift. She had been told not to mix with the boys whose car it was,' Carol replied.

Jane, as we later found out to be her name, was a very good communicator. At the end of her message she said to me, 'will you tell Carol I've got her little boy and he's gorgeous.' I relayed this to Carol and after a few moments silence, by now quite emotional she said.

'Yes, my baby boy died just after Jane he was a month old.' I told Carol that Jane was looking after him, that he was doing very well and that they both loved her. This seemed to make Carol feel a great deal better.

Just after questions in the second half a very strange message came through. I pointed to a lady in the middle section seats and said,

'I have George here and he keeps on saying Dad, it's Dad.'

'Yes,' came her reply, 'George is my Dad.' After giving her more details about her father, his passing and personal family details, I relayed to her, what he was adding.

'He tells me that he knows about Paul and the market stall and he's not happy about it,' I said. There then came a rather abrupt 'No.'

'Oh yes,' I said, 'he's insistent.

The lady shook her head and refused to accept what was being said. Maybe I'd misheard or got a crossed message? I thought. During this time I hadn't noticed another lady, who was sitting next but one to the first, putting up her hand.

'Paul,' she said, 'I think you're with me. My husband is called Paul and he works on a market stall.'

'Well I can't make it fit,' I said, whilst turning towards the first lady. 'This is that lady's father and I'm sure the message is for her.'

'Well she is my friend and perhaps her dad was talking about my husband?' I refused to let the lady take the message and so I asked the first one to think about it.

A few weeks later when I'd been shopping in Doncaster, I bumped into an old friend who had been at that meeting in Rotherham. She told me that she knew the group of ladies, one of whom had refused this message about Paul and the market stall.

'You know I'm sure I was right,' I said to Pam.

'You were,' she replied, 'that first lady was having an affair with Paul who worked on the market stall and that was Paul's wife who tried to take the message.'

I just laughed and thanked the spirit world that I hadn't pursued the message. Normally I wouldn't have let it go but we were getting to the end of the evening and I wanted to try and get around as many people as possible. Pam told me that the lady had apparently said that the message was remarkable but it had frightened her so much when we started delving, that she said she would never go and see a medium ever again, even though she was absolutely convinced in the afterlife.

I often tell people this story at the beginning of other meetings and I always get to see quite a few scarlet coloured faces! It's no wonder some people will not speak up at meetings I think they're sometimes frightened to death, even though there is no death, that we might uncover some dark secrets of theirs and then tell everyone all about them.

Well I can assure you, more often than not the spirit world will tell us these things in a coded fashion (and that is only if they need to be spoken about), so only you are able to recognise what they are talking about. After all you know your people a lot better than anyone else and so you know that they would never willingly embarrass or upset you, especially once they've passed over. It's just that they like to give you as much proof as possible, to let you know that not only are they alive and well, but they are also still very much interested and informed in your lives.

Janet and I went on to do another five meetings together. One event was organized by Edlington Spiritualist church.

Gail and Paul Buckley had just taken over the booking secretary's job. One Saturday morning they called round to see Daz and myself to ask if I would take a meeting for them at the local community centre. It was Paul's suggestion as he knew that I'd taken many public meetings before and he also told us that the church would be too small for an event of this nature. As Janet and I were already working together I thought it would be good for her to come along.

Over a hundred people packed into the small community hall. I was full of cold and I couldn't hear myself think, let alone hear the spirit world talking. I looked at Janet rather nervously.

'Would you like to go first again?' I said, 'because I haven't got anything and this cold is getting no better.'

'Well, alright then.' She said, adding, 'I think I'll take my shoes off on the platform because they're too uncomfortable.' Without realizing what I was saying, I added,

'Oh don't do that Janet, I can see you falling.' Gail was in the room and she looked at me in surprise.

'Give over Paul,' said Janet.

'Well don't say I didn't warn you,' I quipped.

As we walked out into the hall I felt a warm sensation around my ears, nose and throat. When we took our seats I was suddenly aware that everything was quite clear. No blocked nose or sore throat, no stuffy head either. In fact I felt on top of the world. Janet went first as planned. Before she got up, she took off her shoes. Whilst doing so she turned around and grinned at me.

She started off very well indeed, people were accepting the messages some of them sounding very astonished. It all seemed to be flowing very well. About half way through her demonstration, Janet said,

'I just feel as if I should step down onto the floor.' With that she promptly put her foot out to climb down from the platform. Almost immediately, Janet literally shot across the floor and under the first row of seats. I burst out laughing and so did everyone else. With tears rolling down my cheeks, I looked at Janet.

'Don't you dare say it,' she said with a scowl whilst picking herself up. I couldn't resist,

'I did warn you.' I smiled.

Janet hadn't realized that the floor had been highly polished and so when she stepped onto it with the aid of her tights it was like an ice skating rink, resulting in her giving us an impromptu display. Fortunately, the only injury Janet sustained was to her pride. The rest of her demonstration went marvelously because the laughter that she'd created had helped everyone to unwind a little.

During the interval we had a cup of tea in the ante room. The minute I walked in my head was thick, my nose stuffy and my throat sore again. I felt twice as bad as what I had earlier.

'I've done my bit,' Janet said quite cheerfully.

'You certainly did,' I said, 'especially the Fan Dan Go.' Janet just scowled and Gail tried to contain her laughter.

I sent a thought out to the spirit world asking them for help to get through the meeting. As we went back into the main hall everything cleared up again and I started to feel quite good.

One lady got a message from her mother, who went on to tell the rest of the audience about some things that were kept under the lady's pillow. Everybody fell about laughing. Another was told how much she'd paid for her phone bill. Her father said,

'She paid one hundred and seventy three pounds and twenty three pence, and she still won't give it a rest.' The woman agreed while the audience were in hysterics. Everything was coming together nicely and the people were having a wonderful time.

Towards the end of the meeting I sensed a little boy who told me that he'd drowned.

'I'm getting the name of Alan, and I believe he passed through water, he drowned.' A little lady towards the back, nervously put up her hand.

'I believe he's about two, or three.'

'It's my grandson,' she said, 'he was three when he drowned and his name is Alan.' Alan went on to tell his grandmother what had happened.

'I climbed through the hole in the fence and over the backs to the pond I was playing and I fell in.'

Alan's grandmother confirmed the details and by this time the audience were listening quite attentively. As each part of the message was relayed I could hear the occasional gasp.

Alan gave some more family details and information about himself and at the end of his message he gave me another name.

'He's telling me.., it's either Davies or Davidson.' The whole audience gasped, his grandmother replied,

'His name is Alan Davies.'

As I found out from Gail and Paul, after the meeting, quite a few years previous, Alan Davies had gone missing from his grandmother's house one afternoon. The police and the whole village of Edlington co-ordinated a search for him fearing that he may have been abducted. Paul, who was at that time a CB Radio fanatic, had organized a group search. As it transpired Alan was found in a pond at the back of his grandmother's house. He'd gotten through a hole in the fence and somehow managed to fall into the water.

Of course most of the people in the hall had remembered the incident as Edlington was apparently a close knit community. Alan's mother unfortunately was unable to attend the meeting but Esther, his grandmother said that she would pass the message on.

Some days later, Alan's mother, through one of the people who'd attended the meeting, asked if I could give her a sitting. I was glad to be of help. I discovered that she was heavily pregnant so I suggested that I visit her in her own home.

Sure enough Alan came back and told his mother many things. She seemed as happy as could be expected considering the circumstances. As I felt Alan drifting away he showed me a teddy bear,

'Mummy's washed it and put a peg on his ear.' I relayed this to his mother and she stared at me in shock.

'How did you know that?' she said, 'I washed it this morning and pegged it out on the line, by one ear.' To add to everything else this clinched the message for her.

I have always found that when the need is the greatest, the messages from the spirit world are quite remarkable. I've often said that I believe I work better in a public meeting as opposed to a spiritualist church. Some might not have agreed but I'm sure it's true. I always think that the people in a church are convinced of the after life, although it might not always be the case, whereas the people who attend the public meetings are not so aware.

Usually at the start of a meeting I ask for a show of hands of newcomers. You can almost guarantee that about ninety percent of the audience have never seen a medium before and the other ten percent have. What's even more odd is that you can fill a hall or theatre quite easily with five hundred or so people but go along to a spiritualist church and you're lucky if you get fifty in. Yet if the church put a charge on the door they often get a full house.

I think there are two reasons for this. The first is that people probably feel more relaxed in a theatre maybe because it doesn't have the trappings of a religious meeting house and secondly, it's as if people value what they're having to pay for and it seems the more they pay the more they value it. Despite this, as we know it, money plays no part in spirit communication. It doesn't matter how much we give in material wealth what counts is how much we give of ourselves.

That night in Edlington those people gave a lot and the message from Alan Davies helped to convince many of them because they all knew of the situation, they'd all in some way helped in the search for him and so the spirit world repaid that kindness by enabling Alan to talk with his grandmother, in detail, in front of them, giving them all knowledge and comfort.

I was asked back to Edlington many times by Gail and Paul, who have since become very good friends of ours. Funnily enough one evening Alan's mother came along. She was pregnant again and during the first few minutes, she had to be rushed out of the hall by Paul and his friend Dennis and taken to hospital, where she later gave birth to a beautiful bouncing boy.

Incidentally a few months later, I'd heard that Rotherham Borough Council had agreed that meetings of mediumship could take place in the borough's buildings. After all they'd leased them to the Christian outreach group on many occasions and I pointed out that it was only fair that we were able to use them. However, they did increase the charges of the Arts Centre, perhaps it was because they could see the popularity of the meetings and realized there could be some money to be made, who knows?

The meetings we did at Rotherham after that went down very well. On two occasions at least fifty extra people offered to sit on the floor as all of the seats were full. We weren't supposed to let them in but I couldn't turn them away. We did manage to find a few seats, but others just sat around the stage and on the floor. They were quite happy just to get in.

Those meetings were fantastic. The people were absolutely marvellous and so enthusiastic. I think that the Christian Outreach groups' actions, had taken a reverse effect. All of these people wanted to see what this 'Devil', Paul Norton looked like. They wanted to know what all of these bad things I was supposed to be doing were, adding to that all of the people who already knew of me and suddenly we were faced with more people than space to accommodate them. We never heard from the Christian Outreach group again, but they did become involved in arguments with organisers of psychic fairs which were often held in the town obviously not realizing that they were encouraging, rather than discouraging people form attending them.

Daz and I always have a little chat after each meeting and so these gave us plenty to talk and have laugh about. Daz was originally in the Salvation Army. Not by choice, but because his foster parents were officers of it. Before that they'd apparently been methodists and at one point Daz's foster father had been a Spiritualist, but because of his new found vocation he couldn't accept the spiritualist way of thought. I could sense this a lot, when I used to take Daz to visit them in Sheffield, so I made a point of not discussing either subject.

When Daz was in the home one of the staff befriended him and started taking him to the Catholic Church. He was eventually confirmed but as he told me later he was trying to find a way in life and he'd only really gotten confirmed because he thought that with faith, his disability could be cured in some way.

After I had gotten to know Daz better, I told him about the spirit world and assured him that his physical disability would no longer be with him when he got there. He cried with joy. After all of these years he'd finally found the truth. That being that we do not die, we pass over to the next stage of life, life eternal without the trappings of physical or mental difficulties.

Daz has come along way since I first met him growing stronger each day. He implicitly trusts both the spirit world and myself. The spirit world in particular have proven to him beyond any shadow of a doubt not only that life continues, but that they can help with earthly situations when the need arises. For Daz this is his way of life, full of positive energy and direction, a way that he has thoroughly investigated and chosen for himself.

If he'd have chosen another direction then I would definitely have supported him in his decision. There was no way that I would have tried to sway his thoughts or ideas. Even if I'd have wanted to, I knew I couldn't. Many people believe that I think for Daz. Well I don't. He has a mind of his own and if people are willing and able to listen they will see his brilliant mind come alive. Unfortunately a lot of people tend to look at him from a point of view that because he uses a wheelchair he does not understand.

I know that this applies to a great many people nationwide. Because of some physical difficulty, they are often patronised and treated in a manner which I consider to be second rate. There's an old saying, 'You shouldn't judge a book by its' cover.' It's a great pity even in this day and age that we can't often remember these words. Fortunately though there are people who will gladly listen to Daz and others in a similar position and offer the respect they deserve. One group of people that we met, were advisors at the local mortgage advice centre.

We'd never really considered getting a mortgage but because the rent we were paying on the flat was quite high Daz came up with the idea that we might be able to buy a home for the same amount of money each month. I'd asked the spirit world for guidance and they directed us to an organisation which gave independent advice on a variety of mortgages. It was a very long shot, because my income was quite low and Daz relied solely on his disablement benefits.

George Ball, one of the advisors at the organisation thought that there might be one or two problems but he was quite willing to help us as much as possible. He was very impressed with Daz's determination to succeed in living as independently as possible. George told us to have a look around at some properties. When we'd found one suitable we were to get in touch with him again.

Daz and I scanned the local papers. There were hundreds of houses to chose from. We looked at quite a lot but none of them really fitted the bill. A few months had passed and Daz was starting to feel a little despondent. One Thursday morning I'd collected the local paper as usual, normally I would have had a look through it over morning coffee. But this particular day I had some sittings booked and I wanted to make sure that the flat was as presentable as possible. Daz would often said that people were coming to hear me and not to look at the flat however, we'd had an experience with one lady who did nothing but criticise the decor and furniture. In the end I refused to give her a sitting and told her leave. I did feel bad about it, but she'd annoyed me that much that I ended up in an unsuitable frame of mind to be able to give her a spiritual message.

I put the paper on Daz's tray so he could have a look through it. As I was vacuuming the hallway I heard him shout really loud. I dropped the vacuum cleaner and rushed into the lounge.
'What's the matter?' I asked, quite concerned.
'Look,' he said, pointing with his head towards the paper. He'd been looking at property guide. As I looked closer I could see that there was a bungalow for sale. It seemed quite cheap and it was only a mile or so from where we were already living. I made a note of the estate agents telephone number, gave them a call and arranged to pick up the keys so that we could go and have a look.

Strangely enough just after I'd phoned the estate agents the people who were booked for sittings telephoned to say that they couldn't make their appointment. I had planned to collect the keys in the evening but because of this stroke of luck I could now go and get them straight away. I say stroke of luck, I actually believe that the spirit world had played a part in engineering this situation.

It took us nearly an hour to find the place. We'd driven past it quite a few times. It was so well hidden that we couldn't see it from the road. At the front there were two garages, one of which belonged to the neighbour. Adjoining the garage was a six foot high fence which we discovered went all the way around the bungalow. From the outside it looked really nice. There was a large front garden and an even larger back garden. The bungalow had only been built a few years earlier and it still looked very new.

Inside there was a smart little kitchen with fitted units, a very large lounge and dining room with patio doors to the front and rear gardens, a nice sized bathroom and two very large bedrooms. There was central heating, double glazing and who ever had lived in it previously had decorated it in some very soothing tasteful colours.

Daz was really impressed. 'When we move in I can sit in front of these doors. We can do this, we can do that, I can have....' I didn't like to spoil his thoughts so I just agreed. Daz liked the place and more importantly it was ideal for him to live in. That afternoon we contacted George Ball and put the wheels in motion. He called us into his office where we had to complete a load of forms asking a great many questions.

George was very good because whenever he needed to know anything relating to Daz he would ask him. Most other people would normally ask me and I then would tell them to speak to Daz, explaining to them that he was able to understand. Daz was really pleased that he was being treated like everyone else. George told us that it would take some time for a decision to be made, but as soon as he heard anything he would be in touch.

As the weeks passed we received the occasional letter from George asking for certain points about Daz's health to be clarified. The time continued to drag on. The estate agents were pressurising us for a quick completion but there was nothing we could do. We didn't know if we had got a mortgage. In the end they told us that they would put the house back onto the market.

Nothing seemed to happen for weeks. Daz was very worried that the house might have to be sold to someone else. I tuned in to Naiomi and she assured me in her gentle way that it was all in hand. I couldn't just tell Daz that, I thought, so hastily I told him that we would have some positive news by December 7th. I don't know why I'd said it. The spirit world hadn't told me and now I'd definitely put everything on the line. What if I'm wrong? What will Daz do? How will he react? My thoughts were all jumbled up. I just prayed that something would come through.

December 7th arrived. I got up early to check the post. I hadn't had much sleep the night before through worrying about what I'd said. There was no mail at all and as the day went on there were no telephone calls either. I hadn't mentioned anything to Daz in the hope that he may have forgotten. I felt so irresponsible for opening my mouth and saying something that hadn't been confirmed by the spirit world.

It had just turned five when there came a knock at the door. It was our next door neighbour. Apparently she'd been away all day and the postman had put this rather large packet through her letter box by mistake. It was addressed to Daz and myself. I quickly thanked her and rushed into the lounge whilst nervously ripping open this packet. My heart thumping, I opened the folder which was inside and paused for a moment...
'We've got it,' I shouted, making Daz jump with the noise. 'We've got the mortgage, we can have the house.'

Daz was over the moon. I gave a huge sigh of relief. I had been right after all. I mentally thanked the spirit world even though I didn't think that what I'd said had come from them. It came as an early Christmas present for Daz, in fact he said, 'The best Christmas present ever.' He couldn't believe his luck. He'd achieved so much in such a short space of time and here he was again, going forwards in his quest of being able to live life as normally as possible.

Due to the usual element of legalities we weren't able to move until after Christmas. In a way I was pleased because we had so much to do. There was all the Christmas things to get out of the way, all of the packing and arranging of a van. We'd have to write to all our friends and give them the new address. There were just so many things. I often wonder how I kept my sanity.

We spent most of Christmas with half packed boxes scattered around the room. Gyp and Bobby thought it was marvellous with all of these new things to play with. (Incidentally, I had almost forgotten to tell you, we got Bobby as a play mate for Gyp He was one of two farm bred pups which were made homeless. We really wanted both of them but couldn't afford it.) If they weren't in the presents or tinsel they'd be knocking over the boxes or chewing bits of newspaper that I'd used to wrap pots in.

At the time, I couldn't help but notice how Gyp seemed to be putting on a lot of weight. It wasn't as if I was over feeding her, so Daz and I decided to keep an eye on her just to be on the safe side.

With Christmas out of the way we finally managed to move. I must admit even though I looked forward to moving, I couldn't believe how stressful it was all turning out to be. My mind was in a complete whirl whilst trying to make sure that I hadn't forgotten anything. Fortunately some friends of Ian's, (Daz's care assistant), helped us to get moved quickly and unpack most of the boxes.

It wasn't long before we started to get a little more settled. Daz really did like his new home. He said to me, 'This isn't our house, but our home.'

I felt quite pleased that I'd been a part of helping Daz achieve one of his main ambitions. I really did give my thanks to the spirit world for I knew without their help we wouldn't have come this far. Daz's happiness didn't end there.

About a month after we'd moved in Gyp, who was by now very large, gave birth to five beautiful little puppies. Of course I thought that Bobby was too young and too small to father any pups so I didn't keep the dogs apart when Gyp was in season. They both proved me wrong. Now we had seven dogs in the house.

As the pups started to grow, they started to chew. If it wasn't my shoes or Daz's wheelchair foot rests, it was the furniture. Even Gyp and Bobby didn't escape being chewed. It didn't take me long to find homes for four of them, yet no matter how hard I tried, I couldn't find a home for the fifth one. When it was time for the others to leave, both Daz and I were a little sad. Despite the fact that they'd ruined half the furniture we really did love them.

One by one the people called to collect their pups. One lady that we'd met at a church in Nottingham and who'd over heard our conversation about them, asked if she could have one. Daz and I agreed and when it was old enough, we took it down to her. We were then left with Gyp, Bobby and this tiny puppy. He was the smallest of the litter.

'Listen Daz,' I said, 'Let's keep him.' Daz agreed, and so Lucky, as we later called him, (we got that from, Lucky we kept him!), stayed as part of the family. As a precaution I had Gyp spayed so that we wouldn't be having another twenty or so tiny feet running around the house, barking and wrecking everything in sight!

Chapter 7

I was just relaxing watching the television when he caught my eye. At first I wasn't sure then came the voice.

'I'm Allister,' he said with a very big grin, 'and my Auntie Barbara's gonna be there tonight.' I didn't dare move too much in case he disappeared.

'Can you tell me that again?' I asked, just to make sure this was for real.
'My name is Allister will you say hello to my Auntie Barbara?' This time there was no mistaking it.

Margaret Pickering a lady who I'd met in Hull a couple of years ago had telephoned me quite out of the blue. She had since moved to Glasgow and she asked if I was interested in taking part in a week long tour along with herself and another medium called, Irene Williams. I'd never been to Scotland before so the opportunity was too good to miss.

Irene lived quite near to me so we arranged to meet at the railway station to journey there together. Daz needed to stay at home and Ian, one of his care workers, offered to look after him for the week.
Margaret had arranged for Irene and myself to stay at a small hotel in the city centre. When we arrived, she met us at the station and took us to the hotel.

Glasgow was a very busy city which was quite built up. There were a maze of roads for us to negotiate. It was more like being on the famous spaghetti junction in Birmingham. Margaret had no problem finding her way around and of course keeping up with the rest of the traffic. In next to no time we got to the hotel. I was thankful that it wasn't me driving. Even though I'd passed my test I hadn't built up the confidence to travel into Glasgow and after seeing the place I was glad I hadn't.

Because I had nothing else to do I thought I'd watch television after which I'd intended to have a little chat with the spirit world and then a rest. I was doing just that when I saw the vivid outline of this little boy.

'How did you pass over?' I asked him.
'I got an infection in me kidneys.' he replied. He was a lovely little lad with short dark hair and a few freckles around his nose.

I assumed he was about nine years old.
'Actually,' he said in a rather matter of fact tone, 'I'm nine and a half.' I just smiled.
'Well alright then,' I said, 'will you come and tell me some more tonight?' Allister said he would and almost as quickly as he'd arrived, he disappeared.

That evening we were taking a meeting at the Freemason Hall in Edinburgh. We arrived there quite early and with it being a summers' evening we decided to have a stroll down by the castle. I'd never seen such a beautiful place. It seemed so fresh and clean and the castle looked magnificent with it's flag flying high above the tower. The air felt really good despite the heavy flow of traffic.

It was soon time for us to get to the hall and prepare for the meeting, so we strolled leisurely back up the road.

The time seemed to fly and it was by now seven thirty. Margaret demonstrated first. The advertisements had apparently asked people to bring photographs along so that they could be read by Margaret. Although very good what she did wasn't my idea of mediumship. Irene went second. She did blindfold psychometry, which is where a person holds an object and they go on to talk about either it's origin or the background of the person to whom it belonged. Again, it was very good but still not my idea of mediumship.

During this time, I'd been watching from a corridor at the rear of the hall so when it came to my turn I realised that I'd gone and forgotten the contact I'd made with Allister. As I stepped out to the applause I noticed a young man standing beside a gentleman who was sitting right at the back. I pointed towards him.

'I have a young man here who tells me he passed in an accident, it was a motorbike.'
'That's my son,' said the man.
'I'm hearing a name, it sounds like Peter.'
'That's his name.'
'I'm not sure,' I said, 'but he seems to be about seventeen.'
'He was seventeen,' came the man's, by now, emotional reply.

Peter went on to tell his father that he had seen his mother wearing his watch and his rugby shirt.
'She was in my room the other day, Sunday.' He told me. I relayed this to his father.
'Yes that's quite true,' he said. Peter told us more about himself and his family. He was a very good communicator but as time went on, I realised that I needed to make another contact. There was nothing there at first then I heard a familiar voice.
'Barbara's sitting over there.' It was Allister, this time he seemed much clearer.

He guided my thoughts towards a lady who appeared to be alone and sitting about half way down the hall. I looked over towards her.
'The lady that's wearing the white coat.' She looked up, 'yes you my love,' I said as she then looked down at what she was wearing. 'Do you know Allister in the spirit world?' I inquired.

'Why yes.' She sounded quite surprised.

'Then you must be his Auntie, his dad's sister?' I asked.

'I am,' she answered.

'I have Allister with me,' I said, 'in fact, he came to me this afternoon whilst I was in the hotel in Glasgow. He tells me that he got an infection in his kidneys, is that correct?'

'Yes,' came her reply as she wiped a tear away from her eye, 'he died with, kidney failure.'

'He says hello Barbara.'

With that, Barbara just burst into tears. Allister went on to tell his auntie that his dad was supposed to come along but at the last minute he had to cancel because of working commitments. He also told her that he had her dog with him. Barbara was very pleased indeed. She was able to confirm everything that Allister had said.

'I'm named after Dad,' he told me. Again this was true. Allister's father was also called Allister. Towards the end of the contact, Allister reminded me to tell his Auntie his age. I said to her, 'when I was in my room back at the hotel I was thinking to myself that Allister looked to be about nine and he said to me, 'actually I'm nine and a half.' Barbara gasped.

'Allister passed away two days after he was nine and a half. He kept telling everyone that he was that age before he passed.'

It was a very emotional and enjoyable meeting indeed. Margaret had no idea how many people were going to come along. She'd said that the promoters had decided to sell the tickets on the night for most of the meetings. As it turned out over four hundred people had packed into the Freemason Hall.

The following evening we were in Perth then on to Motherwell and Galasheils. Galasheils was a beautiful place on the borders. Despite the scotch mist which I joked about with Irene and Margaret, it looked quite nice. The town was very small indeed and I was wondering if anyone would turn up.

'Don't you think that it would have been better to sell the tickets in advance?' I asked Margaret. She said that the promoters were trying to save costs on overheads.

Nearly five hundred people packed into the Volunteer Hall. I was due to go second. Irene went before me giving psychometry again. As I was standing in the wings I sensed a very small boy. He had very large blue eyes and pure blonde hair.

'Mummy's here,' he said to me, 'she's in red,' he added, 'like my fire engine.'

I knew that red was a popular colour so I thought to myself that I would need something more.

'Can you give me a name?' I asked.

'Pat,' came his reply.

As I looked out from behind the curtains and scanned the audience I was surprised to see only one person wearing red. It was a lady sitting right towards the back of the hall, in the raised seating area. The shade she was wearing was exceptionally bright and noticeable.

When it got to my turn I went out and told the audience what had happened. I then pointed to the lady in red, (sounds like a song!),

'I have the little boy with me again, is your name Pat?'

'Yes,' she replied.

'Then who is Ian?' I ventured. I suddenly felt as if there was air going into my heart.

'Ian's my little boy who died.'

'Well he's not dead my love, because he's talking to me now. Did he pass with some kind of... a hole in the heart?'

'Yes,' she responded enthusiastically.

Ian was able to tell us many things including the fact that his mother had a fire engine made out of some flowers to place on his coffin. She'd also placed a photograph of the family in his hands.

'I didn't want him to go alone,' she replied. By this time most of us were getting quite emotional. I'd noticed a man, standing with Ian, 'who's Robert?' I asked.
'My father.'
'Well can I let you know that Ian's with his Grandfather and not alone and can I tell you that it's your strong love for him that has helped him to come and talk to us today.' It was a very loving touching message. Pat was so overcome with joy.

Another lady's mother communicated to her. I could see the mother sitting in a wheelchair. She told me that she could propel herself and walk a bit but she preferred to have some one else do it. This caused quite a bit of laughter especially when the daughter replied,

'She was an idle so and so.' The mother in spirit agreed.
The meeting continued with a great deal of warmth and humour. We'd all worked so hard to deliver a unique demonstration.
Motherwell and Perth were a little slower in pace though. A couple of times I had difficulties in making the right contacts. We're not always good you know. At times for many of us it can be very difficult indeed and we are by no means perfect either.

Some people tend to think that because we're mediums we have all of the answers. They also seem to forget that we have our own lives as well. We still have to go home and pay our bills and deal with all of the usual family worries. We have to cope with the physical loss of our loved ones as much as anyone else. Perhaps we are perfectly sure about life beyond in the spirit world, but that doesn't mean to say that we can be in constant touch with them day in, day out.

If the spirit world choose not to speak to us or show themselves there's nothing we can do. More often than not they do come through, but then there's times when perhaps we're not well enough or the conditions are not quite right and so we then have to muddle through as best we can. Sometimes with terrific difficulty.

I hadn't been to bed the night before we set off for Scotland I was up all day Friday, all day Saturday and I'd finally managed to get to bed at two thirty Sunday morning. So you can see why I struggled a bit. I know it was self inflicted but it's just one of those things. The difficult part is when you feel that you have to give some kind of explanation, well I mean, what do you say?

When someone is grieving it adds more pressure to the medium. More often than not though, people are usually very understanding and they are often quite willing to come back and try again if need be. Fortunately these times are few and far between.

Glasgow was our final meeting. I'd been a little disappointed that Perth and Motherwell had not been too good but I reassured myself that at least a few people were able to get loving messages. We were appearing at the central hotel. The promoters suspected that it was going to be a good turn out and quite rightly so. Nearly seven hundred people crammed into ballroom of the hotel. Unfortunately there was no ante room for us to sit in so we had to sit make do with a screen at the back of the hall.

Every now and again I popped my head around the screen.
'They're still coming in,' I said to Margaret and Irene. By the time everyone had got seated it was ten to eight.

We should have started at seven thirty. Irene went first. It should have been me but I was still feeling a little tender from the two previous meetings so I made some excuse about going to the men's room.

The moment it came to my turn, I stepped onto the platform and immediately felt the presence of a young man. As it transpired he'd taken a drugs overdose.

'Kevin's my name,' he said, 'Karen's my sister's best friend.' At this point I was guided to a young lady sitting near the front, she had her head bowed.

'I have someone called Kevin. I think he is for you. Are you Karen?' The young lady just nodded. As she lifted her head I could see the pain she was suffering.

I described Kevin's passing.

'He says it happened in London. He was living alone. He says it was a very small dingy bedsit.' Karen nodded in agreement. She must of been so distraught, that she found it difficult to speak.

'It's not her fault,' Kevin told me, 'tell her not to blame herself.' I relayed this to Karen and she couldn't contain herself any longer. The tears came pouring out.

'There,' I said, with a lump in my throat. 'I'll speak to you afterwards.'

The rest of the demonstration flowed and I was really pleased with the results.

At the end of the meeting I went over to Karen and put my arm around her. Still sobbing she told me what had happened. Both Kevin and herself were drug addicts. She was supposed to go and visit him in London and take some drugs with her. For one reason or another, she was unable to go.

By that time Kevin was desperate. He'd apparently concocted his own drug by using sleeping tablets. He'd injected that much into himself that it had caused him to have liver failure.

Karen, although beside herself with grief, did say that she felt much better after hearing from Kevin. It made me feel quite sad to think that this young man was so dependent on drugs that he went to great lengths to satisfy his need thus resulting in him passing over.

Despite this bit of sadness, it was a perfect end to a wonderful week. I'd heard so many mediums say that working in Scotland was difficult and yet I thought it was quite easy. The people were marvellous. I'd never met such warm responsive groups of people as these. I was a little sad when it was time to leave but I was also looking forward to getting home and seeing Daz and the dogs.

When I got back they were all over me licking my face, biting my fingers and generally running round in delight.

I couldn't wait to tell Daz and Ian all about the trip and how little Allister had come to talk to me in my room and then come back later at the meeting to talk to his Auntie. As I was reliving the week Ian presented me with a pile of unopened mail and a list of telephone messages. It was back to the old grind stone again.

Most of the letters were confirmation of bookings I had with churches. As I went through the list of telephone calls I noticed that there was one from Barbara Kelly. I'd met Barbara through Marion Massey. Marion thought that she might be able to help me with my work and so it was arranged for me to go along to see her.

Barbara had a beautiful house in London and to the rear there was a kind of conservatory which housed her office. Barbara and her husband Bernard Braden, were some years before my time very famous television personalities. Barbara used to be on What's My Line and Bernard hosted Braden's week, apparently some kind of consumer programme, along with Esther Ranzen, who I believe was just starting out.

Both Barbara and Bernard were now running their own agency for after diner speakers and such like.

We'd had a chat over some tea and Barbara had said that she would be in touch if anything suitable for me turned up. When I telephoned her she explained that a TV company were making a pilot programme on the paranormal and they had contacted her to see if she knew of any mediums.
Obviously she knew me and so she had put my name to them. They had unsuccessfully tried to contact me whilst I was away and so she gave me their telephone number and suggested I call them straight away.

As it turned out, the producer of the programme wanted me to go to London the following day. Fortunately Ian was still around, so I asked him to look after the dogs whilst Daz and I went to London. I'd asked the television company if they minded me bringing Daz along, because I wanted to take him sight seeing. They had no objections, in fact they thought it was a very nice idea.

We got to London in good time. Our first stop was Wyvern Rogers, the television company. It was right opposite the Duke of York Theatre so we didn't have a problem finding it. As we were waiting in reception this very large jolly chap came in all smiling and chatty.

'Hello,' he said, 'And you must be Paul Norton.'
'How do you do,' I replied.
'I'm Brian Izzard, the producer. 'Well we're just waiting for the others to arrive and then we'll begin,' he said cheerfully, whilst walking off into an office.

As the minutes passed a stream of people walked into reception and then into the office. There was a lady and gentleman, a vicar, an older man and then another man whom I recognised from television programmes.

'It's John Clive,' I whispered to Daz. He was still none the wiser. 'He often plays comedy roles.' Daz nodded. After about an hour and a half I was beginning to get a little tired of waiting. I was just going to ask the receptionist how much longer they would be taking, when the office door burst open.

'Paul,' said Brian in that most enthusiastic tone that television producers tend to use, 'come on in.'

The lady at reception said that she would sit and chat with Daz.

I was offered a seat and introduced to everyone.
'This is The Reverend Graham St. John Willey, Peter and Mary Harrison, Aelwyn Roberts, John Clive...' I smiled and said hello. The minute Brian had finished, each one of them in turn started firing questions at me. It was like being on Mastermind.

'What do you think about ouija boards? I think you are communicating with the devil. I think it's mind reading. How do you feel about these comments? Most mediums cold read people.' I couldn't draw up enough breath to answer them.

I paused for a few seconds and then went on to answer each question in turn and a few more after that. By the time I'd finished my head was in a spin.

'Paul,' said Brian, now even more enthusiastically, 'you acquitted yourself marvelously. You're perfect.'

As Brian explained they wanted to see my reaction to the pressure and of course hear my answers to the questions, so they decided to put me through a kind of test. Fortunately, I passed with flying colours.

'We'll be in touch soon,' Brian said whilst showing me to the door.

When we got outside I told Daz what had happened and we both had a good old laugh about it, after which we decided to go for lunch and then tour the city as planned.

It wasn't until a few weeks later that I got a letter from Wyvern Rogers about the programme. It said that it was going to be called, 'David Frost's Night Visitors.' It was due to be filmed at Cardiff Castle a week later. The letter gave details of where I would be staying what trains to catch and what time to be at the castle for the filming.

All week I was on edge. My mind was creating all of these images, you know, like you see in the movies, 'cut, action,' etc..

When the day finally arrived I checked my case to make sure I had everything I needed. I'd packed four different suits so that I had one which would be suitable, along with six ties and an assortment of different coloured socks. I was only staying over for two nights anyone would have thought I was going for a month!

After a very long train journey, (the train was delayed due to point failure), I finally arrived in Cardiff. One of the researchers had arranged to meet me at the station and take me to the hotel.

When I got to my room, I unpacked my things had a well earned shower and collapsed on the bed. I had the evening free and so decided to go for a little walk around the town to try and find the exact location of the castle.

I didn't have to look far, it was just at the end of the road. There were some peacocks gracefully strutting around the court yard calling to each other and occasionally fanning their feathers for all to see. The castle looked lovely. It had a really good feel about it and I was very much looking forward to getting inside for the filming.

The following morning I got up early, had breakfast, chose which suit I was going to wear and made my way down to the castle. When I arrived there, one of the researchers came over and showed me into a waiting area. She came back a few moments later and took me through to the dressing room.

They'd arranged for everyone to wear evening clothes, because the programme was being filmed as a kind of after dinner discussion, so I didn't need all of those suits, after all. I was dressed up in a bow tie with dinner jacket and trousers.

Sandie, the researcher then took me through to the make up room and handed me over to Elizabeth Russell. There was already another lady being made over, she turned towards me smiled and said hello. I smiled back. I couldn't help but think that I recognised her, so I whispered to the young lady, who was by now smothering my face in some kind of foundation cream.

'Who is that?' I asked.
'Sian Philips,' came the lady's reply, 'she's a well known welsh actress.'
'Oh,' I said, 'I thought I recognised her.' I remembered later that I'd seen the film Labrynth, or at least I think it was that and Sian Philips had played the part of the witch in it.

After being made over I was taken back to the waiting area. By this time, Peter and Mary Harrison had arrived, along with Graham Willey, Frances Ommaney, a television producer, Peter Ramster, an Australian psychologist who they'd especially flown in, Aelwyn Roberts and the singer, Lynsey de Paul.

I'd only ever seen Lynsey on television. She looked so different in real life and she was such a chatty down to earth person making everyone feel comfortable. It was a pleasure to be in her company.

117

We were all there chatting away merrily, when David Frost came into the room and shook each one of us by the hand whilst having a few words with us about the filming.

I was just getting into the swing of things when Sandie came back in with an attractive young lady. There was something very familiar about her but I wasn't sure what.

'Paul,' said Sandie, 'this is Toyah.'
'Hi Toyah,' I said, pausing for thought, 'Toyah Wilcox?' I asked.
'Hi Paul, yes,' came her reply. Well you could have knocked me down with a feather. When I was at school Toyah was often in the pop charts and I had all of her records and posters of her. She was one of my teen idols and now here I was meeting her. I couldn't believe it. I was beginning to feel as if I would have to pinch myself to make sure it was all real.

The only pictures I had of Toyah were ones where she had her hair dyed different colours and spiked. I hadn't instantly recognised her because her hair this time was straight and its natural colour. Never the less all the sounds of her songs came flooding back to mind, its a mystery, I wanna be free, thunder in the mountains.. I could hear them all whilst visualizing Toyah, in all of her dress singing.

Later, in polite conversation I told Toyah that I had all of her records. Although a little embarrassed, she smiled and said she was pleased that I enjoyed her music.

The television company had put on a sit down meal for us. It was much appreciated. There was a wonderful spread accompanying it. I sat in between Lynsey and Toyah. Both of them were very warm indeed. Lynsey chatted about her house in Highgate, London and the resident ghost they had and how she was hoping to move. She told me that she'd seen Doris Collins and how Doris had helped her a great deal.

I told Lynsey how I had become involved in mediumship and how Doris Collins was the first medium I'd seen and how she'd both impressed and inspired me. So we both had something in common!

The programme was to be filmed in three different sections. There was a part on out of body experiences, a part on reincarnation and the last section on spiritualism. In between each section Sian Philips would read some kind of story about a spirit or ghost, or something along those lines. I watched each section being filmed. It was all very interesting listening to the stories each person had to tell and then the 'experts' opinions and explanations.

It got a bit monotonous after five hours of retakes. I was just praying that the section I was in would go smoothly as it was by this time getting late.

At half past nine in the evening they'd finally gotten round to the part on spiritualism. Elizabeth from make up, came along to check that I looked alright.

'We'll put some more on here, I think,' she said as she dabbed some more foundation on my cheeks and nose. She then led me onto the set. Some comfortable chairs and a sofa had been neatly arranged by the fire place in the great hall. I was to sit on the sofa, next to Toyah. Graham Willey was sitting next to me on a stool, there was Frances Ommaney opposite with David Frost and Mary Harrison sitting beside the fire place.

The great hall was breathtaking. There were shields and coats of arms decorating the walls. The ceiling had beautiful wooden beams all the way along it. I could just picture a mediaeval banquet taking place, it was marvellous. Before the filming commenced I was briefly shown a list of forty questions that David had to choose from, to ask me. I had no idea which ones he was going to ask so I sent a thought to the spirit world in the hope of some guidance.

'Are you ready? three two one and action.' The film started rolling. David first asked me to describe what it was I actually did. He then made a few suggestions as to the kinds of people who would come along to see me and the types of messages they would receive, at which point he moved on to Toyah.

She said that she believed fully in my abilities but, she raised doubts as to whether or not people should contact their dead, as she put it, through mediums and spiritualism. I corrected her on two points.

'Firstly,' I said, 'there is no death, there are no dead, secondly, ' it isn't possible to receive messages on demand. We cannot contact the spirit world, they have to chose to talk to us. At this point Graham Willey stated,
'Jesus said in the bible that these people who communicate are not our loved ones but demonic angels.' I was fighting to keep a straight face. Fancy trying to frighten people with this nonsense, I thought. I went on to say, that the bible had evolved over a period of years and had no doubt over that period of time become somewhat distorted. Adding that it couldn't possibly be construed to be absolutely correct in all respects.

I pointed out that the spirit people provided at times astounding evidence about themselves and they almost always poured their love on to their people.
'How can this be demonic,' I said, 'I can see these people they look and act only slightly different from you and I.' Before Graham had the chance to respond, David interrupted with another question.

I say almost always pouring love onto people, simply because not everyone in the spirit world is able to show their love. If they'd had difficulties whilst in the body, it's possible for it to be the same case for them in the spirit world. Do you remember how I said earlier, we retain the same personality? well, the fact is we do. Perhaps in time as we spiritually evolve and progress in the spirit world we are able to show these feelings?

I think it's important to remember that we do not change the minute we pass over. The changes come with learning and experiencing.

I remember once giving a sitting to a lady and her friend. The lady's mother communicated to her and I could sense from the mother, that there was some kind of barrier between her and the daughter. As I listened carefully I couldn't believe what I was hearing.

'You can tell her I still hate her,' said the mother.
'Pardon,' I replied out loud. The mother repeated what she'd said. I fumbled for a few moments to the point of embarrassment, wondering how on earth I could say what I'd heard. I also had doubts as to whether or not it was me, possibly getting it wrong. The daughter was obviously getting impatient.

'Look,' I said, 'I may be wrong with this, so please forgive me if I am. But I'm sure your mother just said that she still very much dislikes you.'
'Are you sure she said dislikes?' came her abrupt reply. By this time, I could feel all my muscles and nerves trembling.
'Well, actually, she said,' I whispered, 'She still hates you.'
'And I do her,' came the daughters' reply, followed by the both of them laughing quite uncontrollably.

As it turned out, the mother and daughter had never got on. They literally, as they both admitted, hated each other. The lady told me that many mediums had given her, her mother, but they'd always said that she was giving love. I'd been the only one to say what I'd heard. She thanked me a great deal, because for her it was the best evidence she could have received.

The filming went on without a hitch so there was no retake for us. By the time we'd finished I was completely drained. A few of the others who were staying in Cardiff and myself decided to go back to the hotel bar, for a well earned drink. Whilst in there, Graham St.John-Willey and myself had a most wonderful chat. Neither of us bore any resentment towards the other and we were both able to understand each other's point of view, whilst agreeing to differ.

I was really pleased because often in the past, people from other religious bodies had usually been extremely closed minded, sometimes down right rude, occasionally violent and more often that not quite unchristian, to say the least. You must realize at this point I am talking about a very small minority and I'm certainly not exaggerating.

At one demonstration I was giving ten people from the born again faith were carted off in a Police van, because they'd literally smashed down the front doors of the venue trying to disrupt the meeting. Of course there was Rotherham where two elderly ladies were accosted whilst trying to enter the building.

Fortunately Graham Willey along with a great many can tolerate others' ideas and ways to God. They may not agree with them but they are prepared to listen and that I think is a very valuable point. There's too much trouble about religion and after all what does it say in the bible?
'In God's house there are many mansions.' So there are many avenues to God.

After a good nights' sleep and another delayed train journey, I was pleased to get back home to the more routine way of life. Wyvern Rogers wrote to me again asking if I could go back to do some filming for a voice over. So a few days later off I went to Cardiff again.

They wanted me to chat to an actor as if I was giving a sitting. I was able to say virtually what I wanted. As it happened though, I did end up giving the actor a message, which he did accept!

Some months later I was sent a copy of Night Visitors. It had already been shown on HTV but because we live in Yorkshire we were unable to see it. I looked forward to watching the finished version and at points I was able to explain to Daz what had been happening, behind the cameras. Fortunately they only cut out a little bit and they gave me a very fair hearing.

This isn't always the case. Often when mediums have appeared on television the presenters have tended to try and make fools of them or they would edit important parts out. In my case, this wasn't so and I was very pleased about the programme very pleased indeed. It made all of the work and travelling well worth while, as well as giving me the opportunity to share yet again the knowledge of the spirit world with other people.

Being a medium, to me means sharing whatever knowledge I have no matter how great or small, with whoever I am able to do so. That's why whenever an opportunity like night visitors comes along I generally take it. You see it gives me the chance to be able to bring something into the lives of people who perhaps wouldn't normally come into contact with the spirit world and share with them the truth that there is no death.

Chapter 8

As I opened the pages of the magazine the words hit me,

'When the medium contacted my fiance I was a bag of nerves.' This was an article in the Sunday Mirror Magazine about a sitting I'd given to a lady at Mansfield, Nottinghamshire.

About three months after the night visitors project I received a call from Barbara Kelly. She told me that Mary Harrison one of the people on night visitors had passed my name onto a researcher from the Kilroy programme and they wanted me to go on their show about the paranormal. I was quite happy to oblige. They asked me if there was anyone who'd had a sitting or message from me who would consider going along to discuss what had happened.

Only a few weeks before I'd gone to Mansfield to do a sitting for Margaret Jones. When I first met her I could see that she was desperate and so I gave her my telephone number so that she could call me and arrange a sitting, which she did.

The sitting went very well indeed and the person who Margaret wanted to hear from came through loud and clear. As it transpired Margaret had lost her fiance. Apparently he'd been burning some rubbish in the back garden, there was a gust of wind and the flames caught his clothes resulting in him receiving severe burns. Kevin, Margaret's fiance, was in hospital and he passed away some eighteen days later. Despite my own losses I couldn't even begin to imagine how this poor woman felt. I just knew that we had to give her some sort of comfort something to keep her going.

I gave Margaret a call and she readily agreed to provide, as the researchers had asked, a testimony of the sitting and so it was arranged that we were to appear on the programme. Margaret was asked to take her son Richard. Apparently he didn't believe what I'd told her in her sitting He thought that either she'd given me clues or I'd gleaned the information out of her and so the researchers thought this would be a good angle to approach the subject.

I was picked up at the station by one of the drivers and taken straight to the television centre. Margaret and Richard were already there in the green room with a host of other people. The programme normally went out live but this one was to be recorded live for the following day. It was soon time to start the filming and we were all asked to take our seats in the studio.

Because I was one of the invited experts so to speak, I was placed on the front row. Susan Blackmore the well known psychologist and sceptic was sitting next to me and next to her was Barbara Smoker from the secular society then Doris Collins and Nella Jones the psychic detective, with Ian Wilson the author sitting behind.

The programme started with various suggestions about the paranormal and spiritualism and then in turn people voiced their opinions. Barbara Smoker soon tackled Doris Collins and then took a pot shot at the medium Stephen O'Brien who wasn't even there. She just wouldn't accept anything at all. She seemed not to have any beliefs in anything. Doris was able to handle her with kid gloves and some of the others who were quite negative towards mediums as was Nella Jones. Author Ian Wilson started off by tearing mediums apart, in particular Doris Stokes.

This was the point of conversation where I became involved. I told Ian that nobody had ever disproved Doris Stokes' work and added that it would have been more appropriate for him to have called her a fraud whilst she was alive then she would have been able to defend herself.

Susan Blackmore interrupted and said that mediums cold read audiences. She said that they would fish around for information and make generalised statements.

'So, would you call a name and address and important personal information generalised?' I countered. She never directly responded and continued to call it cold reading. I never thought at the time I should have asked her to demonstrate what she meant. I think it would have been very good for Susan to give a demonstration of cold reading then one of the mediums to give a demonstration of mediumship that way people would have been able to see the reality, that's of course if she'd have agreed!

Kilroy moved on to Margaret and Richard who were sitting behind me. Margaret gave a very clear account of what had happened during her sitting. It was so moving to listen to her story of tragedy overcome by hope and by the time she'd finished everybody's eyes must have been watering. Richard added that he thought it was all nonsense even though he admitted that his mother, in some way had been helped. Susan Blackmore agreed with him again stating that it was all cold reading and guess work.

After the filming we were all ushered into the green room where they'd put on a marvellous spread. A gentleman who I'd recognised came up to me.

'Hello Paul,' he said, 'I'm Laurie O' Leary.'

'Hello Laurie,' I replied, 'So now I've seen the face behind the voice.' We both laughed. Pauline, who used to sit in the development circle had once written to Laurie telling him about the work that I was doing. I wasn't aware of this till I spoke to him one day back in 1987. At that time he was still managing Doris Stokes' affairs, she had just passed away and so he had many things to do.

We had a very long chat indeed. He talked at length about Doris and it was interesting to hear all of the stories. We agreed to keep in touch and so over the years we had spoken again at length, over the phone. This was the first time I'd personally met him.

'Come over and I'll introduce you to Doris Collins.' He said. So I followed him over to where Doris was sitting. Since Doris Stokes' passing Laurie and Doris Collins had got together to continue the work of promoting mediumship.

Even when not demonstrating Doris Collins still maintained a remarkable presence. Laurie introduced me and I shook her hand and we had a few moments chat. I told Doris that she was the first medium that I'd ever seen and how much her work had inspired me to go forwards. Doris said that she was pleased that she was of some help as she always hoped that her work would encourage younger mediums and that was part of her aim.

Laurie gave me his new telephone number and suggested that I might like to keep in contact, which I have and again we have had many a great conversation about both Doris' and believe me even though I do the work myself I never fail to be amazed at the work that both Doris' have undertaken and their sheer determination and dedication have always given me inspiration.

I said a quick hello to Nella Jones who was deep in conversation with a small group of people and then went on to talk to Margaret and Richard. Robert Kilroy thanked me for being on the show and he seemed very impressed with the way I'd handled the remarks from the sceptics. Despite the occasional negative thrown in by them I'd enjoyed the day. When I got home I told Daz all about it and the following morning both Daz and I settled down to watch the show. It was really interesting to see it from two angles, the part in the studio filming and the part watching at home.

Kilroy was so touched by Margaret's story that he'd decided to write the article about it in his weekly column in the Sunday Mirror Magazine. The headline which was in big black letters stood out the most. The article was divided into two parts, the first was Margaret's story and the second Richard's story. This is what Kilroy wrote.

Margaret's Story.
'When Margaret Jones' fiance, Kevin died on May 24 1991, at the age of thirty four, the 45 year old Nottingham woman was determined to get in touch with him. "I needed to know that he was still around," she said.
"I'd seen the medium, Paul Norton, at the Arts and Leisure Centre in Mansfield and I'd asked if he'd do a private sitting. He came to my house in October last year.

"Before he arrived I said, 'Kevin the one thing that will really convince me that you're still there is if Paul knows you changed your name. That's all the proof that I need'.
"The first thing Paul said was 'Who's David?' I felt like a bag of nerves - that was Kevin's real name. I knew he was in contact with Kevin.
"There were so many things that Kevin told Paul that only Kevin knew. He told me that the shower kept blowing up, and it did. He said that all the clocks in the house had stopped, and they had. He said that Kevin was covered in tattoos - he was. He told me that he used to bite his nails until they bled, and he did.

"There were lots of things that no one else could have possibly known. For instance, Kevin told Paul that a week after he died I had given his new shoes to my brother, Eddie. But before I'd put them in the car, I'd sniffed them to make sure they smelled alright. No body could have know that.
"Through Paul, Kevin has helped me. I was thinking of 'ng to be near my son, Michael, in Chelmsford. I

129

had a session with Paul and he asked, 'Why are you thinking of moving to Chelmsford?' Then he told me the very personal reason that I had for thinking of moving and said, 'Kevin said you are not to go. It's the worst thing you could possibly do. It will all sort itself out soon.' I did as I was told and it has all been resolved, even though I never believed it could be.

"I know that Kevin is still here. My bedroom is like a sauna. It's been like that, ever since Kevin passed away. I have to have my windows open all the time - it's so hot. It's his presence
"It's not just me that feels it. As soon as you get to the door you can feel the heat. The bedroom was his favourite room. We decorated it together.
"I know he's here and I'm quite convinced that Paul can communicate with him. That really comforts me. I used to worry about dying, but knowing that Kevin is there, makes me believe there is another life.

"My 23-year-old son, Richard says that Paul could have gleaned the information from anywhere. That annoys me. It causes trouble between us. He keeps telling me that Paul's a con-man. I get so irate I could hit him - I really could hit him.
"He winds me up a lot. I usually tolerate him because he's my son. If it was anyone else I'd tell him to clear off."

Richard's Story.
"It seemed to me pretty daft. I just thought that she was clutching at straws. I thought there was a logical explanation for everything that Paul told her. He could have picked up things in conversation or made deductions. There are a lot of things related to Kevin in my Mum's house. It can't be difficult for someone to pick up bits and pieces of information. They don't come from the dead.

"I didn't know how he could have known about the shoes and I have to admit that her bedroom is always

hot. I don't know why. It's not that hot anywhere else in the house but it is hot in my Mum's bedroom. I can't remember if it was always like that.
"She used to get on my nerves with what Paul told her. It would be, 'Paul said this, Paul said that.' I just used to turn off and not listen to her. I had an explanation for everything she'd been told, but she wouldn't listen to me.

"I tried to keep quiet because it was obviously giving her comfort. But I wished she would pack it in. I was worried that she would get hurt by finding out that someone was making things up and lying to her.
"I didn't trust Paul Norton and I didn't want her to end up feeling disillusioned and upset. She'd have been shattered. I was also worried that she would be made to look like a fool. She'd told all her friends what he'd said. She told them how convinced she was that he was communicating with Kevin and that Kevin was still around. If Paul was proved to be a fake she would lose face and be humiliated.

"What Paul told her did comfort her. It gave her a lot of hope and she felt secure that Kevin had not gone off and left her on her own.
"That's why I didn't come straight out and say that it was all rubbish. I just tried to imply that it could all go wrong. I was only trying to prepare her.

"Paul used to argue with me constantly. I told him it was all nonsense. I said there was only one way that I could be convinced that he was genuine and that the day he came up with it, I'd change my mind.
"It was something that only I knew. When Kevin was in the Chapel of Rest and we went to pay our last respects we went in one at a time. When I went in I put my hand in the coffin and stroked the side of his face. I didn't tell anyone what I'd done and no-one saw me do it.

A couple of days later Paul said that he'd got proof for me. He said, 'You told me that there was only one thing that would convince you. Kevin knows what it is. He's going to tell me.'

"He said, 'Did you put your hand into the coffin and stroke Kevin's face?' I was speechless. I knew nobody else could have known. Now I have a different view, although I still find it hard to believe that we can receive messages from the other side. But I do understand now why mum is so convinced." '

Richard and Margaret have become very good friends. We often speak on the phone and when we do you can guarantee that there is usually some underlying reason for me phoning them. It's almost as if the spirit world have wanted me to call to give Margaret reassurance. Nowadays although Margaret still feels low occasionally she seems much stronger and able to cope with life's obstacles. I am only pleased that together the spirit world and I have been able to reach yet another person and touch upon their heart and soul.

A week or so after the Kilroy programme had been screened I received another call from Barbara Kelly. Radio 4 were doing a programme called 'Ad-Lib'. It was to be hosted by Robbie Robertson. The producers had seen me on Kilroy and they were apparently impressed with what I'd said. They asked Laurie O' Leary to put a group of mediums together to discuss mediumship. They told him that they wanted me on the programme and he'd said he would try and arrange it.

We all met at Broadcasting House in London one very cold January morning. I'd just gone through the doors when I literally bumped into a gentleman who was on his way out of the building.

'I'm terribly sorry,' I said.

'No it's my fault,' came his reply as he was walking off to a waiting car. It turned out to be the former Prime Minister Edward Heath. I did feel a little embarrassed because I then almost literally bumped into Dennis Healey MP who was also on his way out and to coin an old phrase, I felt like a 'silly billy'.

Waiting in the foyer was the medium Glyn Edwards with Gordon Higginson, the President of the Spiritualists' National Union and Doris Collins. I said hello to them all shook their hands and went to sit down. At first I felt a little inferior. These top mediums were there and I'd been asked to join them. I think I was scared because they'd had so much more experience than I'd had. A short time later Laurie O'Leary came into the foyer with the Danish medium Marion Dampier-Jeans. I'd never met Marion before but I had read articles about her in the *Psychic News*. It was very interesting talking to her.

Once together we were taken over to a studio in another building where we were introduced to Robbie Robertson. I'd remembered his name but I couldn't put a face to it. Once I saw him though I realised who he was. He used to host the television show Ask the Family. I'd remembered watching it when I was younger.

Robbie was very warm and welcoming. He explained that he wanted us all to discuss mediumship and occasionally he would add questions to our conversation. It all seemed pretty clear to me. Of course a medium has to be a good talker so you can imagine when we all got together what it was like. No one else could get a word in edge ways!

Robbie asked where the spirit world was and how it worked. Gordon went on to explain the various states of consciousness and Doris added that she wasn't exactly sure how it worked for her, but she was aware that it worked and very well. Robbie suggested that the messages were a little trivial.

I interrupted and explained that we were not liable to talk of major events just because we'd passed over unless of course this is what we did when in the body and for most us because we retained the same personality, it would be likely for us to talk about somewhat ordinary situations that to some, would perhaps seem mundane.

Doris went on to tell Robbie about a sitting that she'd given to an American lady emphasising the fact that what appeared to be a mundane message to other people turned out to be quite remarkable for the lady concerned, as it had apparently transformed the lady's whole life.

Robbie, who was still quite inquisitive, asked whether or not we should deliver predictions. Marion Dampier-Jeans said that it should not be done in a spiritualist church but sometimes in private sittings, there could be a need. Gordon added that this was called psychism and not mediumship.

Gordon then spoke a little about physical mediumship where spirit people could manifest quite visibly to those present and where the voices of the spirit people would be audible to everyone. Robbie seemed a little taken aback by this but accepted Gordon's explanation.

The conversation went on for well over an hour and we'd all enjoyed discussing various experiences and opinions. Laurie had arranged the group so that there was a mixture of both young and not so young mediums and this seemed to form quite a nice discussion giving everyone the opportunity to see both old and new points of view.

Without thinking I'd mentioned how the Spiritualist's National Union had refused me a Class B Membership, an individual membership of the Union, and yet they'd still taken my money. Something which I was very annoyed about. Robbie asked me what their reasons were. I told him that they hadn't given me any because, as they'd said, they were a Limited Company and they didn't have to.

Gordon, who was sitting next to me raised his eye brows. He was the President of the Union, which I'd just had a go at. I saw this look on his face and I thought I was in for it. Afterwards he asked me to explain the circumstances which I did. He promised that he would look into it as he wasn't sure what had happened and he would get back to me. I'd also asked him about an advanced mediumship course which was being held at the Arthur Findlay College, Stansted Hall, Essex.

Stansted Hall was left to the Spiritualists' Union, by Arthur Findlay, who wanted it to be used for spiritual advancement. Regular courses for developing mediums and healers are held there. Gordon was also the Principal of the College. He inquired as to why I was asking about the course.

'Do you wish to come along?' he said.

'Yes, I do,' I replied.

'Well don't pay anything,' he said, 'you can come along as my guest but you'll have to work hard. We'll also pay your expenses.' I thought that it was very nice of Gordon to offer and I gladly accepted.

When the programme came out on the radio they'd cut quite a lot of things out. It was obvious that they'd edited it but never-the-less, it all sounded very good. I'd expected them to remove the part I'd said about the Class B Membership of the Spiritualists' Union, but much to my displeasure they hadn't.

Of course by this time, I was getting quite used to speaking on television and radio so I was pleased that I'd come across quite confidently. I think it's very important because people are more likely to listen to what is being said. After all not everyone can speak up in public. Some of the very good mediums stay relatively unknown. This I think, could be one of the reasons why. Generally their private sittings are very good but they do not have the confidence to take public meetings or appear on television and radio.

I told Daz all about the recording and that Gordon had invited me to Stansted Hall. He was very pleased for me and I promised that he could come along to the college for the ride and to see what it was like. I did feel a little guilty about my dig at the Union, especially after Gordon had extended the invitation for me to attend the Advanced Mediumship week.

However, he was not in the least concerned, in fact he thought that it was important for me to speak up and he did promise to investigate the situation. I decided that whatever the case I'd certainly try my best when I got to the college.

Chapter 9

It was a glorious August afternoon the sun was shining, the birds singing. We'd been on the motorway for over two hours when we saw the sign. 'Stansted Mountfitchet three miles.'

'Well its not far now,' I said, turning towards Gail, Daz and Ian.

I'd asked them to come along for the ride. Gail had already been to the Arthur Findlay College before with her husband, Paul. Daz and Ian hadn't and I'd promised them at the beginning of the year when Gordon had invited me, that they could come to see what it was like.

I'd seen various postcards of the college but believe me they were nothing in comparison to the real thing. This beautiful building was set amongst acres of grass and trees. We parked the car and decided to have a good walk around the grounds as it was so nice.

Gail obviously enjoyed herself. She was like a tour guide.
'This is the Sanctuary and that is the famous tulip tree,' she said pointing across the neatly lawned gardens. The tulip tree had a special place in the hearts of everyone at the college. Apparently it had been known to give off various powerful vibrations. Some mediums, as the stories go would openly go out to the tree and give it a big hug. I could see why. It was beautiful in all respects and I must admit it did seem to give off tremendous natural power.

After a very quick tour we made our way to the main entrance of the building. There, sitting on one of the benches, was a rather sad looking lady.
'Hello,' I said with a smile. The lady only barely managed to answer. I assumed that she was one of the lecturers but I couldn't help feeling that she was very

low. So I sent a thought out to the spirit world for her to receive the help she needed.

Glyn Edwards was in the foyer. He came rushing over shook our hands and took hold of one of my bags.

'Hello again Paul you're in the medium's quarters,' he said, rushing off towards some stairs. The medium's quarters were towards the back of the college. The best rooms overlooking the car park were taken up by Gordon, Glyn and a medium a who I'd heard of, called Eileen Roberts.

My room was overlooking the housekeeper's flat and the goods area. It was quite small yet sufficient enough for me. We put my things on the bed and let Glyn show us around. He asked if we would like a cup of tea and some biscuits.

'That would be nice Glyn,' I said, 'We didn't have the chance to stop on the way down.' We decided to go downstairs so that we could sit outside the sanctuary where there were some chairs and tables. It was such a lovely day that we didn't want to out miss on the nice weather.

Gail started to get the giggles as Glyn was walking over with our tea. I don't know what it is about her. Ever since the first time I met Gail and Paul, Gail would often burst into fits of laughter for no apparent reason. She has such an infectious laugh that it often sets everyone else off. So naturally I started, then Daz, then Ian. Poor old Glyn wanted to share the joke but non of us knew why we were laughing. He left the tea for us and said he would see me in the dining room at six o'clock.

After Gail, Daz and Ian had left, I decided to go back to my room and unpack my things. It must have taken me about twenty minutes to find the mediums' quarters. I tried almost every door on the landing and each corridor looked the same to me. I finally had to go back down stairs and ask Marion, the receptionist for directions. It turned out that I had to pass through the kitchen to get to the back stairs leading to where our rooms were.

When I got back up stairs I walked straight past the mediums' lounge towards my room. As I was doing so I heard a voice.
'Hello.' I froze for a second, thinking that the spirit world were very clear indeed.
'Hello,' came the voice again. It seemed to be coming from where the lounge was. I walked back towards it and popped my head around the door. 'Hello, I'm Eileen Roberts, you are?' It wasn't the spirit world after all.
'Hi, I'm Paul Norton.'
'Oh yes,' she said, 'Glyn said you was here.' We exchanged smiles and I said that I must go and unpack my things.
'Of course dear,' she said, 'we don't want you looking all crumpled.

By the time I'd finished unpacking I had about twenty minutes to spare before tea. I decided to get a quick bath and change of clothes and made my way to the dining room. I couldn't fail to find it because there was a loud murmur of voices coming from behind this very large door. Glyn was sitting at the top table just behind the door along with Judith Seaman, another medium and Eileen Roberts.
'You can have any seat Paul,' he said. Being nosy I sat right next to the wall so I could see everyone in the dining room.
'You know that's where Gordon sits?' said Glyn.
'Oh I didn't,' I replied, 'I ought to move then.'
'You're alright Paul,' he said, 'he doesn't arrive until tomorrow.'

Dinner was very nice indeed. It was placed on the table in serving dishes. There were three courses and it really was very nice. Glyn had us all in stitches. Apparently he was often at the college and he was obviously sick and tired of the same meals week in, week out.

'Oh not frozen food again,' he said, 'I don't think I can stand it any longer.' We all laughed.

After diner we were all to meet in the library where the lectures for the week and the programme of events were to be discussed. Glyn introduced us all and explained that Gordon would be arriving late Sunday evening. He went on to discuss the weeks' events after which most of the students made their way to the bar! We all had to go upstairs to the mediums' lounge to divide the students into groups. Gordon had left instructions that I was to 'shadow' Glyn so that he could show me how the lecturers' worked.

I thought I was going along to learn more about mediumship like the other students. As it transpired Gordon had got different plans for me. It was his intention to have me teaching and lecturing, providing that I was at the required standard. This made me very nervous indeed especially when Gordon arrived Sunday evening.

He seemed, as I found out later to have this habit of dropping things on you at the last minute. He told me that I would be doing a number of test sittings to make sure that my mediumship was at a good standard.

As it turned out I had five sittings to do. The first lady was from Switzerland. Her father communicated a nice message to her. The second was a Swedish lady called Annika Langlet. She didn't say very much at all and her face seemed expressionless. At the end of the sitting, I just smiled and said, 'I hope it's been alright for you?'

'Yes, it was very good indeed,' came her reply. I couldn't believe it, she seemed very impressed.

There then was a couple of English people, in fact they were from Yorkshire so we were able to have a chat about the area afterwards. The last sitting was for the lady who I'd spoken to on the day we arrived, the one who'd been sitting alone outside. She still looked quite sad. As I started the sitting I sensed a young man of about eighteen years of age. As it turned out this was the lady's son. He'd been killed in a car crash in Bombay, India, the place where the lady lived. By this time she was crying. He was able to tell me his real name and nickname and where and how he was killed and personal details relating to him and his family.

It was quite a remarkable sitting because I couldn't speak a word of his language and so now and again when I couldn't get my tongue around the words I would ask him to spell them in English. Towards the end of the sitting I felt the need to give the lady a big hug. As I did so she stopped crying for a few moments.

Afterwards she told me that she felt for those few seconds when I'd hugged her, that it was her son and this is what had stopped her crying. She went on to say that other mediums had given her a message from him but no one had given his name or nickname. She was so overwhelmed with comfort.

All of my nerves about doing these test sittings had by now disappeared. I couldn't thank the spirit world enough for helping me. Gordon had gotten to hear about the sittings and he was very pleased that I'd done a good job.
'I knew you would do well Paul,' he said, quite knowingly.

That same week BBC Television were filming an 'Open Space' programme about the college and spiritualism. Gordon was to be filmed giving a demonstration in the sanctuary. Right at the last minute he'd decided that Glyn, myself and another medium would join him on the platform. Keith Surtees, the other medium and myself were to give one message each and Gordon and Glyn were to give three each.

It was bad enough doing the test sittings but a demonstration? I wasn't sure what was the most nerve racking, being filmed or demonstrating in front of Gordon. Everyone knew he was a brilliant medium, that was part of the reason for his nickname, which was God! To make matters worse the sanctuary was packed full and I had to sit right next to Gordon on the platform. I didn't think I was going to manage a single sound, let alone a message.

I went first and fortunately the message was quite good in fact I could have carried on if they'd allowed me to. Keith followed, then Glyn and finally Gordon. It all seemed to fit together like a jigsaw puzzle. I didn't even notice the cameras or the sound man rushing around with this large microphone. The Spiritualist's National Union had got editorial control over the filming so I knew it would turn out to give a reasonably positive impression of mediums and spiritualism.

The rest of the week sailed by and on the last day Gordon came into the dining room for breakfast and tapped me on the shoulder.
'Now you're alright for two thousand week, aren't you Paul?'
'Pardon,' I said.
'You are going to come along?' He wasn't so much asking, more of telling.
'Well, err, I can manage three days.....'
'Good,' he replied. Two thousand week was another course to be held at the college in November and I'd obviously been co-opted to be involved. I did say that Gordon had this habit of dropping things on people at the last minute and this was certainly one of those times.

I did go to the college for three days during two thousand week. Apparently Gordon had given me a very big build up. He'd mentioned how I'd appeared on the television and radio, about the article that had been in the Sunday Mirror Magazine and also that he thought I was a very good medium so when I arrived, there was a buzz from people who wanted to know more about me.

There were many tutors on that week so for the three days I mainly moved around from class to class. On my last evening Gordon had arranged for me to give a demonstration in the library with two other mediums. He again gave me this marvellous build up.

'Paul is a very good medium,' he said, adding, 'But not as good as some of us.' The audience fell about laughing. Unfortunately the demonstration didn't go down very well. Afterwards Gordon came across to me.

'You know I have seen you better Paul,' he said rather cheekily. I just glared at him whilst uncomfortably agreeing.

Before I left the college that evening Gordon collared me in the foyer. 'I want you to come on Physical week,' he said.

'Really?' I replied.

'Now do you think you can make it for the whole week?'

'I'll certainly do my best,' I said.

'Well I'll give you a call in a few days,' he said, 'to arrange everything.

Physical Phenomena week as it was called, was always fully booked up in advance. Usually during the week Gordon would give a demonstration of physical mediumship. This entailed him going into a trance like state and then if the conditions were right a substance called ectoplasm would be produced and the spirit people would use this to materialise in front of everyone and speak so that all present would be able to hear and see them quite clearly. I'd only ever read about these types of meetings and even then I wondered whether or not it was really possible. Not doubting the mediums, but more so the possibility.

Gordon telephoned me as he had said and I jumped at the chance of attending the college during this week. He told me that he was going to be late arriving and asked if I would arrange the students into groups, along with two other mediums, Eileen Mitchumson and Muriel Tennant. He also wanted me to chair the introduction session and a lecture which was being given by Jean Bassett, the publicity officer of the Spiritualist's Union.

When I arrived I was greeted by Muriel and Eileen. They were such a bundle of fun, in fact more like a comedy duo so warm, welcoming and funny. Together we arranged the groups and organised the first evening's activities.

I'd never chaired a meeting before and the strange thing about it, I was more nervous than I had ever been for any demonstration. There was so much to remember, all of the introductions, the apologies from Gordon, all of the activities. Fortunately I got through everything alright. When Gordon arrived he asked me how I'd got on. I'd remembered what he'd said to all of the students on advanced week, about being positive.

'Oh marvelously Gordon,' I replied.
'Was he Eileen?' Gordon asked, whilst grinning at me.

'Yes Gordon, it was wonderful.'

The week was full of various groups, circles and lectures about physical mediumship. It was all new to me and really very interesting. Not only did I have a group to teach but I also had to arrange private sittings for the students with the other mediums and myself. In all I had twenty five to fit in somewhere along the week.

On the Sunday evening Gordon approached me in the dining room.
'You'll be doing the service tonight with Haydn Clarke,' he said.

'Who's going to give the address?' I asked.
'None of you,' came Gordon's reply, 'I shall chair, you will give the clairvoyance and Haydn will be doing psychic art.'

This was and hour before the service. I'd never worked with a psychic artist before although I had seen Gordon work with Coral Polge who is a very famous psychic artist.

Haydn and I got together to discuss how we were going to work. We didn't really have much time what with finishing dinner and then getting a wash and change. Haydn had decided to use an overhead projector because of the size of the sanctuary. I suggested that I would feel better if we could both start working simultaneously, rather than me waiting for him to draw the first picture as he'd suggested. Haydn agreed.

The sanctuary was packed full. My legs trembled as Gordon came into the small lounge.
'Its time,' he said, 'Now you'll both be very good, that's what they've told me,' he added, referring to the spirit people.

After the usual hymns and prayers Gordon gave us a wonderful build up and then left the rest of the meeting in our hands. The minute I got up Haydn started drawing and I made my first link.

In next to no time it was flowing from one person to another. I'd got so wrapped up in what the spirit world were giving to me that I had gone way ahead of Haydn. About three quarters of the way through the service I paused for a few moments to allow Haydn to catch up with me and talk about some of the things he'd got. When it came to the last message it all seemed to start off very well and then it suddenly started to slowly fade.

To fill in a little I glanced at Gordon turned back to the audience and said, 'Do you ever get that feeling that you are being watched by God?' Everyone burst into laughter including Gordon. As I told you earlier he was affectionately known as God. This laughter helped the atmosphere and I was soon able to finish off the message. At the point I was closing I struggled a little bit. I turned to Gordon. 'Do you think you can help me a little?'

'Yes,' he said, 'That part of the message is for the gentleman sitting next to the one you are talking to.' Gordon went on to tell the man correct personal details and as it transpired, the part of the message was for the other man.

After the meeting many people came up to Haydn and myself and congratulated us on a first. One gentleman, Mike Scott, came to me and said that he thought what I had given was very good indeed. As Gordon told me later, he very much respected Mike for his honesty and knowledge and he said that if he had complemented my work then it must have been very good, adding,

'I told you, you were going to be good, didn't I? You see I was right, I always am!' He made me laugh. So you now see where I'd got my twenty five sittings from. I could have had more but because of organising other activities and my group, I just couldn't fit them in.

The highlight of the week was Thursday evening. Gordon had agreed to give a demonstration of physical mediumship. Haydn and myself prepared the library for the meeting. Ensuring that it was completely free of dust and blacking out all of the windows. Haydn set up a recording and sound system, so that everyone would be able to hear quite clearly. A red lamp with a dimmer switch was to be used as Gordon had insisted on one.

Before the meeting Gordon had been strip searched by a couple of students who were chosen at random. He wore a lose fitting shirt, a pair of trousers and some slippers. The library was packed full. All of the people had been asked to remove items of a metallic nature and they were checked for tape recorders and cameras. This was to ensure that there would be no sudden noises which could possibly be harmful to Gordon.

I was to sit on the platform next to Eileen Mitchumson, along side the cabinet, which Gordon was using to sit in. We were not more than twelve inches away from it. Apparently a small space, such as a cabinet is ideal for this type of mediumship as it enables the power to build up more easily. This was a three sided cabinet with a curtain across the front.

Gordon took his seat. All of the lights were turned out whilst he went into a trance state. After about six or seven minutes his guide, Choo Chow came through very strongly indeed. He asked for the red light to be turned up. He spoke for a few moments then guided a still entranced Gordon into the cabinet. There was the sound of clear voices, talking simultaneously, then the voice of Cuckoo, Gordon's young helper stood out.

'Paul,' she said quite clearly, 'You better come and get this.'

I looked at Eileen, she nodded. Shaking a little I stood up, turned towards the cabinet and leaned forwards. The curtains were open and I could clearly see Gordon in a deep state of trance with his hands clasped together, resting on his stomach. There was no movement from him at all. I heard a rustle and then the clinking of metal. Right before my eyes I could see Gordon's belt coming off his trousers, with the buckle end, which was quite large, going through each eye last.

There was no doubt that the spirit world were taking his belt off. As it came out towards me I held my hands closer. It was like a steel rule, a solid form. It all came out in a solid and as I reached for it, all of a sudden it went quite soft and coiled up into my hands. I shuddered in amazement. Physical mediums are not supposed to wear any form of metal whilst demonstrating. This is because the power that is generated is so intense that it can cause and injury to them.

I sat back down for the seance to begin feeling shaken at what had happened. There was a muffled sound of voices, which soon started to get clearer and clearer. They seemed to echo in the whole room not coming from any particular direction. The voices were crystal clear and as they got louder a faint glow started to appear near Gordon's neck. It grew larger and larger, flowing to the floor like a soft yet penetrating mist, building up into the form of a person.

It turned out to be a man. He started to talk to his wife giving absolutely marvellous evidence of a great many details. I couldn't believe my eyes, there was this solid form of a spirit person who looked very solid and yet didn't, if you know what I mean? His voice echoed throughout the library. (Apparently, as I found out afterwards, Haydn had removed the sound system before the seance had started as it wasn't working properly.)

As the seance went on other spirit people materialised. Some were clearer than others. An American lady received a message from her brother who had passed over. He gave completely full names and addresses from the past. His American accent was so clear and precise. He spoke of his mother's illness, giving the exact location and name of the hospital she was in, in New York. He told his sister that his mother would be joining him the following March.

The whole seance from start to finish was truly remarkable. Poor old Gordon was so exhausted that he had to go straight to bed afterwards. There was quite a bit of doubt about the authenticity of that particular seance and there were various comments passed.

Fortunately many of these did not reach Gordon, as we knew he would have been so hurt by them.

In the *Psychic News* which followed, Mary Leiter the American lady who received the message from her brother wrote a letter to the editor, detailing the message and stating that her mother had in fact passed over in March as her brother had said. I spoke to Tim Haigh, the editor of *Psychic News*, and told him about the experience with the belt, however, nothing was ever mentioned about it. It annoyed me that so many people were unsure of the seance and yet the evidence was irrefutable.

A few weeks later, just after Christmas I spoke to Gordon. He was disappointed with the comments that people had made in the *Psychic News*. In fact he was very hurt indeed. He told me how he'd been unwell over Christmas and how he was due in Blackpool for a long week end but didn't feel up to going.

'I shall have to go,' he said, 'I can't let them down.' Gordon said that he would see me at Stansted in early February for the first week end course.

Sadly, Gordon passed over a few days later. He'd returned from Blackpool and at around lunch time. When he got home he had a heart attack and passed. suddenly. His physical presence is sadly missed by many. I have been back to Stansted, once, just after he'd passed yet, that feeling you got within, whilst there, wasn't there at all this time and I've heard many people say the same since. Gordon worked tirelessly travelling both in this country and abroad spreading the truth that there is no death, we do not die. He will be remembered for his tremendous efforts along with the many other pioneers.

I know beyond any shadow of a doubt, that Gordon helps me and I'm sure a great many other people too. It was his way to teach the younger mediums. He has given me absolute personal proof of his help and detailed information, that I have had to check, to do with himself and his family background.

It's such a comforting thought to realise that Gordon and other pioneers such as Doris Stokes, Estelle Roberts and many other mediums are helping the cause from the otherside. They are working as hard now as they did when in the body, giving teaching and providing evidence that there is no such thing as death, it's merely a case of moving from one state of mind, to another.

That last week at Stansted, with Gordon and the materialisation, has meant a great deal to me. I often feel that I was guided to the seance. After all, if I hadn't of met Gordon at the radio station, I may never have asked him about the advanced week course and so I probably wouldn't have gone, resulting in me not being invited to the physical phenomena week.

Chapter 10

It was just after Gordon's passing that I started to feel somewhat low in myself. He had great plans to mind which were to involve the younger element of mediums, including myself. Those who took over from where he left off however had other ideas. Including the younger mediums was not part of them. It was as if it had become a select clique for a very select few.

During this period of time our old friend Sam became very ill with cancer and was admitted to hospital. There was nothing that could be done it was more a case of waiting. It was so sad to see him there gradually getting worse. Each time we visited him he would say.
'When I get out of here Paul, we will do this, and that...' Everyone except Sam knew how bad he was and that he wasn't going to get better. After about eight weeks the inevitable happened and Sam passed over.

Sam had been a good friend and teacher to both Daz and myself. To me in particular. He was like a second father. He would offer guidance on both life and spiritual matters. I can still hear him to this day..
'That spirit world is a load of old tinky tonk,' he would say.

His passing made me feel even more isolated within myself. I wasn't sure whether it was me getting older or whether there was a sudden surge of people passing over. Every friend I spoke to seemed to have lost a loved one. It started to become more of an occupational hazard. We were beginning to wonder who was going to be next. We didn't have to wait long.

The saddest passing we had to experience was that of Daz's nephew. Bradley was just seven months old when his father found him in his cot, he'd stopped breathing. Despite being rushed to hospital they were unable to resuscitate him. Daz's foster father had telephoned me with the news and I had to break it to him. For about ten minutes after the call, I just wandered around the house. How on earth do I tell him that the nephew he was so close to and loved dearly, had passed over.

In between these thoughts I was trying to come to some kind understanding as to how it could happen. I knew so many elderly people who prayed to be taken because they were either ill or had some kind of disability and here was one of the most beautiful little children any parent could hope for, snatched from their loving grasp. I felt so cold.

I got Daz up. He was his usual smiling self, I managed to strain a grin at him. As I was dressing him he asked who had telephoned.
'It was your Dad,' I said, 'He phoned about Bradley.' Daz's smile faltered a little.
'There's no easy way Daz,' I said, 'Bradley passed over this morning.' Daz burst into floods of tears, I couldn't take anymore and joined him. We both sat there crying. I tried to be strong for him, but it was impossible. I knew Bradley as well and he was a cheeky chirpy little fellow. The last time I'd seen him he was racing around the house in his baby walker.

As the day went on I managed to get into some kind of composure. I had to do for Daz's sake. He calmed down a little and we talked about Bradley and some of the funny things he used to do. Daz's foster sister and her husband had given Daz a photo of Bradley for Christmas, so we got it out found a really nice frame for it and placed it on the wall at the end of Daz's bed, so that each morning when he got up, he could see it.

Because of Bradley's sudden death there had to be a post mortem. This added more distress to the family and Daz. They just couldn't bear to think of him being hurt. I tried to calm Daz by telling him that whatever they were able to find may in some way be of help to other babies and small children.

Daz wanted to go and see Bradley in the chapel of rest. I wasn't so sure I did, but went along for support. We'd bought a few flowers and a soft toy for him to take on his journey. Daz felt comforted that he would have a toy. Bradley's parents had dressed him in his favourite clothes. He looked so peaceful as if he were asleep.

There were a lot of people at the funeral. It was one of the most saddest occasions I'd ever come across. Bradley's father carried the little white coffin into the crematorium. He looked so pale and drawn. Because they were in the Salvation Army, one of the Majors took the service. The most heartbreaking point was when we all had to sing Brahms Lullaby. Everyone just cried. For many, it brought back the memories of our loved ones. The heartache and upset surrounding their passings, but nothing anywhere near as sad.

As we sang the curtains at the altar began to close until we could no longer see the coffin.

I couldn't even begin to imagine how Bradley's parents were feeling. I know I felt somewhat inadequate at the time. I knew the hurt of losing someone close, but I couldn't comprehend the pain of a losing a child. All I could do was send my thoughts out to both Bradley and his parents.

Because of the way I'd been feeling beforehand, Bradleys' passing seemed to tip me over the edge. I felt so low that I decided enough was enough. I didn't feel that I could responsibly continue the job of being a medium any more. After all if I was feeling so low how could I possibly help others to lift themselves up? I decided it was time to finish altogether.

I told Daz what I wanted to do and he thought it might be for the best. I wrote letters to all of the organisations that I had bookings with, I cancelled all of my sittings and I had our telephone number changed and made ex-directory, to make sure that there would be no contact with anyone or anything remotely connected to the spirit world or spiritualism.

It was all a bit of a rash decision but I really felt inside that I just couldn't continue. I'd experienced so many negative things from people and there had been so many negative things happen to both Daz and myself. Our life seemed to be going round in complete circles. Just as we thought things were getting better there would be something take place that would overshadow the positive. I had no energy or enthusiasm to go on and I knew that I couldn't possibly help others when feeling this way.

Daz and I agreed that we wouldn't mention anything to do with spiritualism or the spirit world and so we set of about a routine way of living. In the evenings instead of going to a church or friends, we would go out to the local pub for a nice quiet drink or stay in. Occasionally we would contact Gail and Paul but this wasn't often, simply because they tended to mention spiritualism and we really didn't want to know. We were getting along quite happily and there had been no mention of anything spiritual.

One evening, it was in October, we'd just had tea when the telephone rang.
'Hello Paul,' said the very loud recognisable voice at the other end of the phone.
'Now what's this I hear about you giving the work up?' It was Glyn Edwards. I was stunned at first because I had no idea where he'd gotten our number from. When I'd changed it I took the added precaution of asking for it to be ex-directory.
'That's right Glyn,' I said.
'Well you can't just give it up,' he replied adding, 'You're an excellent medium Paul, what do you think Gordon would say?'

I told Glyn that I wasn't really bothered and how I'd felt so tired inside. I explained to him how we'd experienced all of these negative feelings and what had been happening.

'You really need to keep away from people who are negative,' he said. 'They're no good for you. Those things that have happened come to all of us at some time. You must continue, please reconsider Paul, the movement needs you.'

I said I would think about it and thanked Glyn for his concern and calling.

I must admit it was a really nice gesture. Glyn was so busy but he'd taken the time out to call me with words of positive encouragement. He bothered to make that effort which some of our closest friends, didn't. It never made any difference though, I still didn't feel like returning to the work.

Time seemed to pass by very quickly. We received the news that Daz's foster sister was expecting. We were both so pleased for her. I told Daz that she would have a little girl and we looked forward to finding out later on in the year.

Five months had passed and both Daz and myself were quite happy. For the first time in ages we had the opportunity to do the things we wanted to do like staying at home in the evenings and giving our dogs much more attention, or going out if we wished. There was none of the rushing around getting ready for church or public meetings, no missing meals and not getting home until the early hours, everything seemed quite nice and peaceful. We'd not given any more thought to spiritualism or Glyn Edwards call.

A friend of ours who'd lost her husband kept in contact with us during this period of time. She was alone and despite everything that had happened to us, we knew she needed and would value the friendship. She called us one morning to say that she would have liked to have seen Doris Collins, who was appearing at Sheffield City Hall that night. I had no idea that Doris was there and to be honest I wasn't really keen on going. I knew Val couldn't get there alone, so I decided to take her. At least it would be an evening out, I thought.

Daz was spending the day at Bowmer's and there were still some tickets left for the meeting. It all seemed to fit into place nicely, so I didn't mind going along.

We got to the City Hall quite early to make sure we could get a seat. I was still feeling quite low.

'Cheer up Paul,' said Val, 'It might never happen.' I just smiled. When it came to going in, I didn't want to.

'We'll be late,' said Val, taking me by the arm and into the hall. There were quite a few people there, a lot of whom I knew personally from the various churches around the area. Many of them spoke to me and they all seemed so pleased to see me yet disappointed that I had finished the work.

Doris Collins was the first medium I'd ever seen. I had the good fortune of being on both the radio and television with her. When she came out onto the stage she looked so different from the last time I'd seen her. She seemed to give off this immense aura. Despite my feelings I couldn't help but notice it. The atmosphere seemed to become instantly charged as she started to speak.

The messages flowed from one person to another. All of this time inside I could feel a kind of pulling sensation as if I was being drawn onto the stage along side of her. Of course I didn't go onto the stage or even leave my seat for that matter, but I could feel this immense magnetic energy. After the interval Doris gave some more messages and then she moved onto the healing. As she did so, the feelings just kept on growing, like a flower bud opening inside of me. I felt as if I was going to burst. By the end of the evening I was in a buzz, all I wanted to do was join her and work. I was literally amazed at this complete turn around in my thoughts.

Afterwards, Doris stayed on stage to sign some of her books that people had bought. I could see Laurie O' Leary over at one side so I went over to say hello. Laurie shook my hand and beckoned me onto the stage to meet Doris and her husband, Philip. Philip was very jolly and chatty indeed. He had wonderful sense of humour. We chatted for a while until Doris had finished signing the books. I knew she would be tired so I decided on a quick hello. I told her how much I'd enjoyed the meeting and how it had made me feel. Doris gave me a hug and kiss and said that she was pleased to be of help. I felt quite elated.

On the way to Barnsley to pick Daz up, I made a snap decision. I decided that it was time to get on with the work again. As I made up my mind for the first time in over six months, I felt Naiomi's strong and yet secure presence. I knew then, that I was doing the right thing. Val was very pleased for me. She said that she thought there was a reason for going to Sheffield, other than seeing Doris.

When I told Daz he was over the moon. I'd later discovered that he didn't really want me to finish the work, as he thought I was good at what I did. He suddenly came out with all of these plans to organise some meetings and start taking sittings again.

That evening I decided to have a chat with Naiomi. I apologised to her and the spirit people for cutting them out of my thoughts. She seemed very understanding, as if she knew there was a reason for me stopping. Granted, after ten years I needed a bit of a rest. But six months seemed to me quite a long time for a holiday. In any case I'd had no intentions of starting back to work. I had or so I thought, made up my mind.

Word soon spread and a whole host of bookings came flooding in. People started to telephone us after hearing the news and offering congratulations. I wrote a letter to the *Psychic News*, outlining my reasons for giving up the work and how an evening with Doris Collins had inspired me to go forwards with strength. It appeared in the letters page and a few weeks later, there was a letter from Doris thanking me for my kind words and saying that she was pleased to have been of help.

Another lady who'd once received a message at a meeting I'd given in Derbyshire, wrote a lovely letter stating that she wished me success with my work and her message had provided wonderful evidence for her at the time she received it. She emphasised that I must continue the good work I was doing.
Just when I needed the support the most, I received it from many quarters.

When it came to taking my first meeting, I was a little nervous. Perhaps I'd be rusty? I thought, What if it didn't work? There was no need for me to worry because it all went very well. In fact I felt it was the best I had worked in years. Afterwards the whole congregation gave me a tremendous applause. I'd never known this happen before.

The rest had obviously done me good in many ways particularly with my work. All of those negative thoughts and feelings were placed firmly to the back of my mind. I 'browse' through them now and again taking a long hard look at every minute detail, so that I am able to come to some kind of understanding about them and then use them as a positive way of reaching the souls of others.

I often listen to some tapes I recorded of Gordon's lectures at Stansted. They are so enthralling. He tells stories of his life and how his mother, who was a well known brilliant medium, would make him work so hard, to become a better medium. He would say.

'Mother used to tell me never to be satisfied, that way I would always seek to improve and I have done!' The stories always brought laughter, I think it was the way he told them.

One thing that Gordon was always insistent upon was that you can never give up the work and go back to how you were before. This statement was so true. As Daz and I had found out. We avoided everything to do with the spirit world, that was until a friend who was in need sought companionship. We gave her the help and into the bargain we ended up being pulled, like a magnet does a pin, right back into the thick of things.

Once involved in it all again we found it difficult to imagine life without our dear friends both in the body and of course the spirit world. Choose whatever has happened they have never let us down and have always stood by us through thick and thin, positive and negative and I'm sure they always will. The most marvellous aspect of it all is the fact that when we had chosen not to continue the spirit world never once told us that we should have gone forwards. As always they watched over us, knowing that quite soon we would be back on the right path.

One of the first sittings I did, after starting back was for a lovely lady who'd lost her mother. Apparently, her mother knew she was going to pass over and a few hours before she did whilst laid up in a hospital bed, she wrote this lovely poem...

Life is such a precious thing, to know this one has to be ill. 'tis a pity this we do not know
when ours cups we begin to fill. We take too much for granted yet life is full of riches.
Your one true love and your family are first and foremost of all, your brothers and sisters are
second in line and then come your friends one and all.

These are to keep you going, the others belong to God, like the Gold and Green of natures path for many a time we've trod.
These precious times are in God's diary, never to be forgot. They are all waiting in heaven, the walks, the people, the lot.
No matter what happens today my love, let us not despair, remember in heaven we'll have it again it will all be waiting there.

As I read the words over and over they never fail to bring a lump to my throat. They remind me of all of those people who have left this physical world and moved on to the next stage of life in spirit.

As you can see being mediumistic doesn't necessarily protect us from the negative aspects of life and it certainly doesn't exempt us from the emotions felt at the loss of a loved one. Yes, we know they have moved on to a world far greater than this one but, we still do miss the physical presence, the cosy chats and of course the cuddles from them.

Our abilities give us the courage and the strength to continue in life passing on the knowledge there is no death. You see physical life is rather like being at school. We are here to learn and to teach others. All of this understanding then forms a major part of our life in the spirit world. Our purpose I believe, is all mapped out before we are born into this world. Some even believe that we choose a specific pathway before we come here, but, I'm not so sure about that. What I do know is that whatever situation we are in, be it positive or negative, it is all part of the learning process.

Perhaps now you can see why it hurts when we come across those people who constantly tear us apart. We try our hardest to help and guide them, not to run their lives but to, give them strength and comfort for the future. Our aim is simple, to prove that there is no death that life continues beyond the demise of the physical body and that it is possible, when the conditions are conducive to receive accurate comforting messages from those who have moved on. We too, know the trappings of grief so there's no way we would pray upon people's sadness, as we are so often accused.

Some people with a scientific background have tended to try and find equally scientific answers as to what is happening. I wholly agree with this providing they are open minded. Susan Blackmore the renowned psychologist who I met on the Kilroy programme and who is constantly featured in many debates about the paranormal as they call it, has on many occasions stated that once your dead, your dead. To her life is totally extinct at what is called death. She admits to having had a number of extraordinary experiences but believes that they were part of the imagination.

My question is, how does she know that death is the end? More importantly, can she, along with the many other sceptics prove that death is the end? I think not.

People might say, "How can you prove there is life in another dimension?" Well, to me the answer is simple. We are able to convey messages sometimes with absolute accuracy and often giving details about a person or situation which the recipient has no knowledge of. If they have no idea about the information given, then it has to have come from somewhere and to my mind there is only one answer, from the person communicating, the one who has passed over.

Scientists would no doubt say the recipient could have had some sort of subconscious knowledge about the information, but even then, many facts that they simply could not have known will often have been relayed to them. It's not a case of trying to convince or convert, its merely stating our case in open realistic terms.

Unfortunately in our line of work there are those who wish to make a fast buck and yes it is true they can set up as a medium or anything else for that matter, without having to undergo any training or testing or pass any examinations. The Spiritualist's National Union run education and training courses preparing students for public work, however they are not currently nationally recognised or are they a requirement to practice mediumship, or at least not publicly.

The charlatans pray on other people's loss and sadness. There is very little that can be done about them unless they break the law, then there is the Fraudulent Mediums Act which can be used to prosecute fraudulent mediums. But could you imagine having to prove a medium is fraudulent? I should think it's near on impossible.

As genuine mediums we all can and do make mistakes we are not infallible, so it would be very difficult to draw a line between genuine mistakes and intentional deception. My advise to people, is to seek those mediums who are recommended by either friends, neighbours or spiritualist organisations like the *Psychic News* or Spiritualist's National Union. I'm not saying that those who regularly advertise in local and national newspapers are not genuine but it does give rise to serious thought as to why they should have to advertise, in the first place and it's usually every week.

I remember the time I was offered a job on one of the infamous 'dial a medium' premium rate chat lines. The lines at which you are charged a lot more than at the normal rate. I'd originally given them a call to see just what it was all about and to find out what these mediums were like. The lady at the other end of the phone put me on hold for what seemed an awful long time in fact I was beginning to worry how much the call would cost. After a while I was put on to one of the mediums who gave me a 'reading.'

It was pretty much run of the mill stuff and I ended up giving her more information than what she was telling me. About the only thing she did say that had any significance was that she felt I was a spiritual person. Well, I mean, it's a little to vague to even discuss.

She was so sincere though that we ended up having a good old chat, during which I told her what I did. She went on to say that if I was interested I could have a job and gave me the main office telephone number. I must admit it sounded quite strange to me. Out of mere curiosity I telephoned the manager and he promptly arranged an appointment for an interview. I had explained to him about Daz and he was more than happy for him to come with me.

The offices were in the Salford area of Manchester, a mere stones' throw away from the somewhat notorious Strangeways Prison. In fact the prison was two streets away and you could see its' old watch towers dominating the skyline. It must have been the most foul looking building I'd ever seen, Daz agreed with me. In between some dingy looking warehouses we found what looked like some kind of a storage unit.
'Surely these aren't the offices?' I said to Daz, whilst peering at a grubby sign on the wall.

As I did so the door suddenly burst open, making me jump.
'Can I help you?' said the lady now standing in the doorway, rather abruptly.
'I've got an interview for a job.'
'Well you'd better come in then.' Daz and I looked at each other with raised eyebrows. The lady closed the door behind us sliding across, rather loudly, three heavy duty bolts.

There was a hive of activity inside. Telephones were ringing non stop and people were talking all at the same time. The room was filled with clouds of smoke from those who seemed to be puffing constantly on cigarettes and there was a stale smell in the air. We were shown to a desk where there was a telephone. The manager came over introduced himself and very briefly asked what I did. He then pointed to a form on the desk.

'You can take some calls now and we'll see how you get on. If you do alright you can start tomorrow. You can use the form to log down all of your calls. See the notice opposite?' I nodded,
'You must read that out to every caller.' With that he signalled to a lady sitting at the far end of the room.
'The switchboard operator is going to put some calls through to you now.'

The telephone started to ring quite furiously, I hesitated then picked it up. I looked at the big notice opposite, which gave details of everything we were supposed to say to each caller as they came through to our extension. It was mainly information about the service provided and the costs of each call. After this I had to take down the first name of the caller the town which they were calling from and their age, as well as stating on the form the exact duration of the call. This was something that had to be done for each call.

The first person who came through to my extension wanted, as she said, a reading. I explained what I did and then went on to give her a message from the spirit world. She seemed very pleased with what I'd told her and asked me for my fist name, (which was all we were allowed to tell callers) and told me that she would ring again. As soon as I had replaced the handset the phone started ringing again.

I went through this process time and time again. In about an hour and a half I must have taken some fifty calls. My mind was buzzing. I was able to give each caller a little bit of something but as I thought, nothing particularly worthwhile. The manager seemed impressed with the way I'd handled things so he offered me a job there and then. What puzzled me was the fact that he hadn't even bothered to test my abilities or arrange for someone to supervise the calls I was taking, or ask for any references. Because I wanted to know more I accepted his offer. He told us to be there for two the following afternoon.

We just couldn't believe the set up. There must have been twenty odd phones in the room and each one was constantly ringing. Some of the people had tarot cards spread on their desks others had rune stones and crystals. All of them appeared quite confident in what they were doing.

The following afternoon we got to Manchester early and went straight to the offices. Because I had time to spare I decided to have a chat with some of the other 'mediums'. As it turned out many of them had just set themselves up doing card readings. There was only one who mentioned the spirit world. To my mind this organisation was leading people astray. They were advertising mediums when really people were given readings, not messages from their loved ones. After all the job of a medium is to convey messages from the living world beyond not give futuristic readings about love, luck and money.

The company also operated what I can only describe as a sleazy chat line. This was in the room upstairs which was even more dingy than the one down. Some of the girls who had worked on the chat line had suddenly become instant mediums and they too had set themselves up as practitioners. I asked one lady how long she'd been working and was surprised at her answer.

'I bought these yesterday,' she said pointing to a pack of tarot cards. 'I've just done ten readings this morning, its simple.' I went downstairs somewhat dismayed and told Daz what she'd said and what other services they were providing upstairs. We both felt quite uneasy about it all.

I decided to stay at the line for a week. It got no better in fact, much worse. The funny thing was we discovered there were two people who held Spiritualists' National Union, (SNU), awards and another who was in fact the president of a Spiritualist church. None of them seemed to have any idea just exactly what it was they were doing.

Strangely enough they all had pseudonyms. I explained to Daz that it was likely that if the SNU found out, they would have their awards revoked and I should think there would be one or two questions for the one who was a President.

We became quite well acquainted with many of the workers and it had become apparent that to them, it was a living. In many ways this was understandable. But to just set up without proper training, teaching and supervision, I thought, was quite a dangerous thing to do. Not physically dangerous but morally, especially for those innocent callers.

The problem is that some people hang on to every word a medium, reader or who ever else, tells them. It's an extremely responsible job. You have to be so careful. You have to be able to judge whether or not you feel the person is able to receive a message and understand it. You have to make sure everything is perfectly clear and that there are no misunderstandings, especially when dealing with vulnerable people, as many are. That's why I like to record each sitting I give, not just for the persons' peace of mind, but also mine. There are mediums who refuse to allow taped recordings of sittings, I always begin to wonder about them when I hear of this.

Cases such as those on the telephone lines give all of the psychologists clergy cause for concern about some sort of psychological damage that may be caused. That's why, they always bring this subject up when discussing spiritualism. To an extent I agree with them, however they have a tendency of generalising and often they refer to it as 'spiritism' and 'dabbling with ouija boards and things'. As we know, none of these form any part of mediumship or spiritualism. But because of unscrupulous organisations, such as the one to one line and individuals, we all get drawn into the same grouping.

I got paid a pittance for working six twelve hour shifts and taking somewhere in the region of over four hundred calls, which were worth considerably more than what I had been paid. We only went along to see what they were like and after we had found out that week was more than enough to last us a lifetime.

I cannot emphasise enough, that if people are seeking a contact with the spirit world, they should try and find a reputable established medium. There are a great many who take services, every week end in spiritualist churches and if they are free, I'm sure that many of them will do sittings. The other way, which I personally think is the best one to find a medium, is by word of mouth. That way you're likely to have heard it from a person who has experienced a sitting first hand.

I always say that there is a medium for everyone but not one medium for everybody. I know in some of the sittings I've given, they've not all been marvellous, in some cases quite the opposite. But if I am unable to provide what the person is hoping for, I always try to pass them on to someone who I think may be of more help to them.

Whatever the case I always tell them to remember it's not what we wish for, but what the spirit world feels is right for us and is able to provide at the time.

Its very strange because its as if they are aware of things to come. They let us know about the rough patches in life and then they seem to take a back seat and allow us to follow through the pathway. When we've reached the end of a particular cycle, they draw very near to us offering their guiding influence yet again.

I've heard many people voice anger and dismay at those in the spirit world because they feel they haven't been helped in the way they thought they should be, or because things haven't gone according to their plan. Unfortunately the trappings of a material world start to infiltrate the spiritual mind and cloud thoughts. It's as if people's demands upon the spirit world become more materialistically related, as opposed to, spiritually.

I like many others have fallen into this trap at times. But through the sheer determination to develop and learn I have been able to climb the spiritual ladder again. Sadly this isn't the case for everybody for their minds are so strong that even the most powerful spirit person has difficulty in communicating with them.

Since I began this quest I have noticed a dramatic change in mediumship and people's perception of it. Unfortunately, it's not all good. I suppose those that have walked this way before me, are saying exactly the same. Suddenly, everyone wants to become an overnight medium. Giving people messages about having their hair dyed or having fifteen pounds in their purse or buying a new pair of shoes.

A lot of people believe things like these to be wonderful evidence when in reality, they are nothing more than facts of life, barely even psychic. If the medium says something like, "Your father is telling me he was with you when the new shoes you bought today broke," or similar, also including facts about the spirit contact, then this does offer more positive evidence.

There was one medium, a local lady, who I thought was wonderful. She could give some brilliant proof of the spirit world, but half way through each message, she would say things like, you have half a pound of butter in your fridge that cost you seventy two pence, or you went into Tesco and was deciding which joint of meat to buy, you bought the cheapest.

The congregation loved these bits but when all is said and done, they are not evidence after all, if both joints of meat are similar, who wouldn't buy the cheaper one? She has now passed over, bless her. Despite these occasional bits she filled in with, I still maintain she was one of the excellent mediums.

When I first started which was only ten years ago, the mediums were of a much higher calibre. They could really touch upon the hearts and minds of all present, constantly proving the continuity of life, with humility, honesty and humour. Nowadays with the exception of a somewhat small minority, it's more like a theatrical show. Mediums waltzing up and down the stage spending seventy five percent of the time telling jokes and slipping little bits of messages in between.

I'm not saying for one minute that the humour should stop. It shouldn't, but perhaps if there was an even balance between the humour and the evidence then, I think it would be far better. We must remember that those people who attend our meetings are seeking the truth and comfort in a message. As mediums, this is our main priority. If we allow their loved ones to draw near and communicate clearly, they themselves will no doubt provide the humour, to show how real and full of life they really are.

I always remember the many lessons that Gordon taught us as Stansted. He would explain in depth not only the workings of mediumship but how to nurture the gift and allow it to blossom at it's own pace, rather than jumping the gun ourselves and trying to have overall control. His teachings would incorporate practical aspects with which he would break things down and explain them piece by piece, until he was sure we knew exactly what he meant.

Gordon really knew how teach. Although he was a brilliant medium, he like many of us, never knew all of the answers. He did however strive towards a greater knowledge, continuing to develop this throughout his whole life.

There are of course many teachers at Stansted who have learned the same and they constantly try to put into practice with their students, all what they were taught. At the end of the day though it all depends on the students' willingness and ability to learn and adapt.

These are just a few of the boat load of trappings we all fall into, sometimes without even realising it. In our quiet moments, it's important to open our thoughts to those who choose to help us from the spirit world. If we ask, they will show us all that we have achieved. It is then up to ourselves as individuals, to make up our minds as to whether or not we feel that we have slightly gone off the beaten track. It doesn't matter what others think or say to us, for only we know the real answer, it's something deep inside that one day, be it sooner or later, we will certainly discover.

Chapter 11

It's always nice to be able to help people, particularly when they have lost a loved one and feel they are unable to carry on in life. Through private sittings that contact of a personal nature can be and often is achieved. The feelings you experience are tremendous to say the least and they are even more wonderful when people let you know not only that things they were unsure about were correct, but also just how much you have been of help to them.

More often than not they find their thanks too difficult to put into words almost as if thanks, to them is no where near enough. My rewards in the sittings are as I've said, to know that they have in some positive way, been of help. That's all I need. Upon reflection in my quiet moments I can then look back with pride realising that all of the pain and pleasure has worked towards the creation of this great positive energy.

It's nice to see over the years that there has been a great improvement in the mediumship. I think it's important to know that we have moved on, as opposed to remaining on the one level all of our earthly life. After all, the idea of knowing about the great spirit is to be able to progressively move forwards.

In recent public meetings and private sittings the progression has been noticed and not only by myself, but others who have known me and the work I have done over the years.

My dear friend, Pam, the lady who I met at my first public meeting and has since become a close friend, commented on my work after seeing me at a recent public meeting. You might think that it would be too easy for friends to give praise. Well, let me tell you. Pam doesn't mince words, if she thinks it's good she'll say so. If she thinks it's alright she'll say so and if she thinks it's terrible she'll say so! Pam thought that there had been a great deal of improvement both in my work and presentation and I valued her comments.

As I think I've already told you, Pam gives readings to people. She uses tarot cards, even though I keep telling her there's no need for her to do so. I have seen the readings she does, improve tremendously over the years. She is so accurate. I always recommend her to people who wish to have readings.

At the beginning of each year, Pam and I always get together. I do Pam a sitting and she gives Daz and myself a reading. In 1994's reading, amongst other things Pam told me that I would be coming into contact with a young lady who had dark hair and whom I had known for many years. She said that I would be of great help to her. She also told me that I would be helping a friend who had lost her husband, the husband being somewhere between forty five and fifty five years old.

At that time I never gave any thought to what was being said, but as the year went on it all became apparent as your about to see.

In May, I was booked to take some services in the South of England. A few days before I left I received a phone call from a young lady who wished to book a sitting. When I asked her how she came to get hold of my number she said she'd called at my mother's house and asked her for it. I thought nothing of what she was saying, only a little surprised that she had called at mum's. Anyway, I booked her in for an appointment just after I was due to return.

When the young lady arrived, I realised that I knew her. In fact, I'd known of her since I was about twelve. It was Joanne Clarke. She used to knock around with some of my school mates. She also lived at the top of our street, that accounted for her knowing where mum lived. Whenever I saw her, I would always say hello and that was about all because I didn't really know her that well.

As it transpired she had recently lost her boyfriend in a freak accident and she was looking for some answers to her many questions and some sort of contact. Fortunately, her boyfriend communicated a lovely message to her, which gave her tremendous strength. With her kind permission I have included a transcript of the sitting as it happened, taken from the tape recording of it. Some personal things have been excluded.

Paul: I have an elderly gentleman here who is talking about two brothers, Peter and Mike.
Joanne: I'm not sure.
Paul: He's got a young man with him. This young man passed suddenly. I feel quite dizzy, as if I'm falling. I can hear rocks and the sound of metal bars, scaffolding?
Joanne: Yes, I know what you mean.

Paul: He's giving me the name of Mark and he's talking about the twenty eighth of... (Joanne interrupts)
Joanne: September. Yes, he is called Mark and that was his birthday.
Paul: His hair is a mousy colour, it looks blonde at the front. He seems to be wearing it back off his face. Its long, in a pony tail. He's talking of his two brothers and a sister.
Joanne: Yes, that's all right.

Paul: He worked outside. I can see old grey buildings and fields. This is a rural area. Someone passed on the 7th of April.
Joanne: It was the 6th of April. Mark was working on a building site. He was converting an old barn. It was out of town.
Paul: They're talking of Mary, Margaret, I'm not sure.

Joanne: Mark's dad, used to call his mother by the nickname of Mary Margaret.
Paul: There is David, his brother? and Steve, to do with work. I feel as if he was trapped, like something has fallen on him, also as if he shouldn't have been doing what he was doing.
Joanne: They were lowering the roof in an old barn. It had been built too high. They shouldn't have had to do that if it had been done properly, the first time.

Paul: He's got a ring and a pair of hoop earrings in his hand, he's giving them to you. He's telling me that he has been with you recently. You went to a house near a canal and railway line. You turned left down an old track, then right. It's a very rural area.
Joanne: Yes, I went to Mark's friend and workmate's house, it is down an old track where there is a railway line and canal, I did turn left then right. He was with Mark when he had his accident. Mark bought me a ring and some hoop earrings.

Paul: He's also taking me down a street called Cherry Tree Road, I'm turning left. Across the road on the right, there is a kind of Green. I am going to number 7, three people live there. There were four not so long ago, but one has moved.
Joanne: That's where we live, mother, father and myself. My brother has married and moved away.

Paul: He's talking about, Keith, Graham, Darren, Stewart and Steve.
Joanne: I know Steve. (After checking, Joanne found out that the others, were Mark's workmates who were with him on the building site, where he passed over. She also discovered that Peter and Mike, the two brothers, were Mark's dad and uncle.
Paul: He's got something else in his hand, it's a photograph. He took it with him.
Joanne: I'm not sure. (Joanne found out that Mark's sister in law had put a photo of his two nephews, in the coffin with him.)

Paul: He says he loves you very much. He's your boyfriend. You were both looking for a house, just before he passed. He's got lots of red roses for you. He wants me to thank you for looking after his mother. I feel a tightness in my chest. It seems as if there is a cut, and then blood. He's just over six feet tall.
Joanne: He was just six foot and half an inch. We were looking for a house, a few days before he passed. In the accident, a rib punctured his aorta valve and he bled to death. I understand the roses.

Paul: You have a double bed in your room. There is a mirror at the end of it. He tells me you've seen him in the mirror. He is also talking about the three newspaper cuttings you have. One of them is the announcement of his passing. He's showing me ashes, he preferred that. A group of people have clubbed together to buy some kind of plaque or something special. I can see a pool table.

Joanne: I did think that I had seen Mark in the mirror, the description of the room is right. I have all three of the cuttings and only one of them, is the announcement. Mark was cremated. He used to go to the snooker club. They all got together and bought a trophy in memory of him. It will be given to the winner of each yearly competition.

Paul: Who's Sandra and Jane.?
Joanne: His sister and sister in law.
Paul: Sandra's expecting.
Joanne: Yes.

Paul: Mark says that he is so pleased to be able to talk to you again. He really does love you. He wants to say thankyou for keeping him alive. You talk to his picture don't you?
Joanne: Yes.

Paul: Well he says you are to talk to him, not the picture. Oh. by the way, it's one that he hadn't seen. You

have copies of it.
Joanne: He didn't get to see them and I do have copies.
Paul: Joanne, will you realise that Mark is only a whisper away, and will you take his love and thoughts. He says he visits you often and he's been touching the back of your hair. Please please know, he will always be with you, both in thought and spirit.
Joanne: Yes, thankyou.

As I discovered after the sitting, Mark had been working on a building site in a very rural area. They were converting barns into homes. The people mentioned were all of his workmates. Steve was with Mark in one of the barns. They'd had to lower the beams because the roof had been built wrong. As they were doing so a newly built wall collapsed. Part of it hit Mark and he was thrown to the floor. This caused a broken rib to puncture his heart and he passed within minutes.

Joanne told me afterwards that she always felt she would lose Mark, it was a fear she had and she used to cry about it, when in his company. She wrote me a little note of thanks.

June 1994

Dear Paul,

After my boyfriend passed away on 6th April this year, I had feelings I have never felt before. As if someone in my head was angry and wanted to tell me something. It felt like someone was shaking me saying, 'it's me, I need to talk to you.'

In order to find out what was happening, I sought out your telephone number and booked a sitting.

Although I have known you for years, having gone to school together, I have not seen or spoken to you since 1982. You couldn't possibly have known what had happened to me in between time. Also, we moved quite a few years ago, from the estate where you used to live.

The details you gave to me about Mark, his family, friends and the accident, were all correct and it has proved to me, beyond a shadow of a doubt, that someone must have told you whilst I was there in your house. That someone being Mark and the spirit world.

It has helped me very much to know that Mark is not dead and gone and he'll be there to greet me, when I eventually pass over.
Thankyou,
Lots of Love,
Joanne.

Pam was right with her reading. I had known Joanne for quite a few years and I had not seen or spoken to her since 1982. She had dark hair and she was in need of a great deal of help. Unfortunately, Pam didn't pick up that the lady who I would be helping, who'd lose her husband, would be herself.

In early November, Pam's husband, Jim was rushed to hospital after having a fit. The day before he'd hit his head at work and it was thought that this could have caused the fit. He was released but asked to take it steady. A few weeks later he had another one and was taken to hospital for a scan of the brain. Sadly in early December, Jim passed away in hospital, before the results of his scan were back from the lab. Jim was fifty six, just over the age that Pam had given.

Since then both Daz and I have been helping her through this difficult period. She has been so naturally distraught. She knows full well about the spirit world but still finds it difficult, as we all do, to be able to understand the situation. What I think makes it worse is that Jim had been given a clean bill of health in a full medical, just a week before he first went to hospital. An inquest into his passing has yet to be arranged and I think that all of this waiting, to know exactly what Jim passed with, has also taken its toll on Pam.

Fortunately to take her mind off things, she has been doing lots of readings and some hypnotherapy sessions. Together, we are all about to start a further developing group, so this will also give Pam something else to help her muddle through.

Daz and I can only hope that things get sorted out soon for Pam, so that she is able to pick up the pieces and carry on moving forwards, knowing that her friends are by her side.

Chapter 12

As the picture started to build up you could make out the features quite clearly. It suddenly became apparent that this was a man who was in his late sixties. I turned to look at the audience and felt quite compelled to speak to a man who was sitting on the second row.

'I'm getting the name of Hutchinson, William Hutchinson and he seems to be connected with your father, is this right?' The man nodded in agreement. 'This gentleman,' I said pointing towards the picture on the screen, is part of the same family.'

'Yes,' replied the man, 'William Hutchinson is my uncle, my father's brother and the picture being drawn is that of my father.'

Haydn Clarke the psychic artist who I'd worked with at Stansted Hall and myself, had got together and decided to do some public meetings around the country. We were at the Civic Hall in Barnsley, for the first meeting. Because of the size of the hall and the packed audience Haydn had decided to use an overhead projector. As he put pen to paper the first picture built up quite nicely and the contact was very good.

'Your father passed away with chest trouble, emphysema, I think, because he worked where there was a lot of dust.'
'Yes that's correct,' came the man's reply.
'He talking about living in Park Street, in the third house along the left, from the alleyway.'
'Yes, that's right.'
'The house and the street no longer exist.' By this time, the man couldn't believe how accurate both the message and the picture were. His father gave him a very evidential message and some practical help with his life.

179

The second link was equally as good. Haydn had began to draw an young child, it was a little boy. He went on to say that he felt this little boy had drowned, because he said his lungs were filling up. As I scanned the audience, I heard a very clear voice and was immediately directed towards the back of the hall to the far left.

'I'm somewhere over there,' I said, pointing in that direction. 'I'm getting the name Gardner, I want Margaret Gardner, who's living in the body, or if you like, she's still with us.' I heard some muffled sounds coming from that direction and a few moments later I saw a hand being slowly raised.

Our friend Gail Buckley had come along to the meeting with us. I asked her if she would pass the microphone around the audience so that everyone would be able to hear what was going on. I could just make her out, hurrying along to the back of the hall.

'Margaret Gardner is my mother, she's not here tonight.' Came a somewhat nervous reply from the young lady who had put up her hand. I asked her if she recognised the picture at all.
'I'm not sure,' she said, 'but I think it could be my brother, when he was much younger. He's passed away, but he didn't drown.'

I asked her if he'd had any problems with his lungs before he passed over.
'Yes, she replied, he punctured his heart and his lung filled up with blood, that was what he passed with.' Haydn and I had obviously made two mistakes, which I thought were allowable considering the circumstances.

Firstly, the picture was of her brother, when he was a child, not a child who had passed away. He was in fact twenty one. Secondly, because Haydn had felt the lungs filling up, we both thought he'd drowned when in fact he'd punctured his aorta valve and this caused his chest to fill with blood. I continued with the message.

'I have three sisters, Elizabeth, Edith and Sarah all in the spirit world and they are talking of Stavely Street.' Jane, the recipient, explained that the three ladies were all sisters in law to her mother and the whole family had originated from Stavely Street.

We discovered, after the meeting, that Joanne Clarke was in the audience with some friends, one of whom was the sister of her boyfriend in spirit, Mark. The message was for Jane, the sister. The family name, which I didn't know, was Gardner. It turned out that Mark was trying to get a message to both Joanne and Jane. The information given was all correct and there was no way that we could have known they were there, because there were so many people, to us, it just looked like a sea of faces.

Another lady received a clear message from her father. He was able to tell her that he'd been listening in to her conversation.
'She's had that blue and grey box out again,' he told me, 'the one with the old photos in. She also took out that big newspaper cutting.'
The lady was quite surprised at what she was being told.
'She spoke on the phone to her friend about the box, the pictures and the paper cutting.' The lady confirmed all of this to be quite correct.

Another young man communicated to his girlfriend. He had been killed in a car accident.
'We went out of control and hit a tree,' he told me, adding, 'It wasn't our car, we borrowed it if you know what I mean?'

His girlfriend laughed, 'He means he stole it.' He showed me a tattoo that he had on his left arm. It was a shield, with a name written on it. I described this to the young lady, she nodded tearfully.

'It looks like the name Tracey,' I said.
'Yes,' she whispered, 'that's right, it's me.'

We were all pleased that the evening had been a great success. Many pictures were recognised by the recipients, along with all of the messages given to them. Haydn had put his phone number on each picture so that the people who received one would be able to contact him to let him know whether or not they had been able to clearly identify the person drawn. After the meeting many people came up asking for details of private sittings and where and when we would next be appearing.

Haydn and I travelled from one meeting hall to next. From Barnsley, to Luton, to Chesterfield and finishing up at home, in Doncaster. In all we had taken fifteen meetings in just three weeks. Each one had been a success. The audiences were all very welcoming and the attendances were much higher than what we'd first expected. Some of the evidence given was quite remarkable.

Daz thought all of this travelling was marvellous, even though we were often home very late. He especially enjoyed the meetings. During the tour he decided that he would be our roadie and navigator. So each time we went out, Daz would be armed with map books, addresses of venues and a computerised mapping system printout of our destination and exact route. The only trouble was, that on the way home, he was usually a little inebriated, to say the least, and often, we got lost because our navigator had, had one too many!

Incidentally, Daz doesn't want you to think he's a alcoholic, he only has a couple of cans of beer a night to help him sleep. The doctor says it's the best thing for him. It also helps keep his system flowing, if you know what I mean!

Daz often mentions the time we gave the work up. He says that he couldn't imagine having to sit at home for the best part of the day, not having any meetings to go to. He also noticed how we'd had more work this time, than ever before. The funny thing was, that there were also quite a number of articles about me in the *Psychic News*. These were certainly a first. They were all well written and came across positively.

When I was on Kilroy, even though I'd had a major part in the discussion, I wasn't mentioned at all in the article which appeared on the front page of the *Psychic News* the following week. Yet this time, my name was mentioned quite frequently. One of the articles was about the message that Jane Gardner had received at Barnsley. In the write up, there was a copy of the picture that Haydn had drawn. Another article was a written piece that I'd submitted to the paper. It was about the time I spent working on the 'dial a medium' line.

A few years earlier, *Psychic News* used to hold quite large publicity meetings in London. They would have a host of what they considered to be the top mediums such as, Gordon Higginson, Doris Collins, Glyn Edwards, Stephen O' Brien and many others including some healers, involved in the all an all day event. They hadn't held one for quite some time and so they thought it would be appropriate to restart these annual events.

Much to my surprise and honour I was asked by Tim Haigh, the editor of *Psychic News*, if I would like to be on the programme, as one of the new younger mediums. I was delighted and accepted. They called the event, 'Mediumship '94' and it was to be held at Lewisham Theatre in London. The date was fixed for September 24th.

For the weeks that followed, there were large adverts giving details about the event and those taking part in it, appearing all around. Some years ago I'd remembered that Pam had said I would be part of a major event in London, which would involve working along side Doris Collins. I'd not thought anything about it, that was until I'd seen the first advert.

Doris Collins was appearing, along with the well known medium Albert Best, a young medium called Mark Brandist, myself and some others which were to be announced at a later date.

I was so excited to be part of the event and so pleased that Doris was going to be there, after all she had figured quite a lot in the spiritual pathway that I had been taking and I thought it was rather uncanny that our paths would meet up again.

As time went on, various articles including individual profiles appeared in the papers. Because I'd worked with Haydn on the other meetings, I thought it would be nice for him to come along on the day, so I gave Laurie O' Leary a call, as I knew he was organising the event. He thought it was a good idea and said that he would let Tim Haigh know. Tim agreed and so it was arranged.

We were to be the first on after Tim had opened the meeting, so I decided to stay with our dear friend, Jean Knight, who I'd met at Stansted some years ago, because she only lived a few miles away from the city and that way I wouldn't have to get up too early to catch a train.

I had told Joanne Clarke about the event. She asked if I would drop her off in London, so she could stay with her friend and then come on to the meeting the following morning. Jean only had enough space for one at her house, which meant I was unable to take Daz along. He had to stay at home with Ian. I didn't mind Joanne coming along as she would be company on the long journey down.

We got to Lewisham in good time. Haydn was already there setting up the projector, along with Laurie who was making sure the stage setting was alright. Tim Haigh suddenly appeared from behind the curtains. He came over, introduced himself and then showed me where the dressing rooms were.

The event was starting at eleven. Haydn and I were to be first, then a couple of other mediums then Doris, with some healing. There was to be a lunch break, followed by a trance demonstration, then another break then Mark Brandist, Doris Collins and finally Albert Best who was to be presented with the spiritualist of the year award.

I really didn't want to go first but we had very little choice. The idea of having to warm them up so to speak, made me feel quite uneasy to say the least. The time seemed to fly by and suddenly we found ourselves waiting in the wings. I must have been so nervous, that I missed Tim's introduction for the next thing I knew we were walking out to the applause.

I said a very quick good morning and moved straight into the demonstration. The contacts came through very smoothly and Haydn was drawing away nicely. When he'd drawn the first picture, he suddenly realised that he'd done it straight onto the screen. He'd forgotten to put the plastic film down first.

'I'll have to draw this again later,' he said. I looked over towards him. It all went silent for a few moments. I quickly made a comment, to the lady who the picture was for,
'It looks as if you'll have to take the whole projector home for your picture.' The audience started to laugh I sighed and we carried on.

Our part had gone down very well with the audience. I realised, afterwards, that I was pleased to have been first, because it gave me the opportunity to sit amongst the audience with Joanne and Jean and enjoy the rest of the day. I did just that.

It was so nice to have so many people working together all for the same cause. The young mediums along side the older ones. It all blended so well and some of the evidence given during the day was quite remarkable.

A couple of weeks later, the *Psychic News* wrote various articles about each of us who had appeared at Lewisham. The headline, for the one about Haydn and myself was, 'Clairvoyant and psychic artist leave audience breathless.' When I read what they'd put, it almost left me breathless!

That article, along with the many others, sits proudly in a photo frame, in our spirit room at home, along with the letters and cards, from the many well wishers and grateful people who we've come across over the years. There's been so many.

Looking back we have known many people who have in some way, experienced great tragedy in their lives and yet through the sheer determination of both themselves and their loved ones in spirit, they have been able to climb over the hurdles of pain and loss, with tremendous strength and courage.

It's a lovely feeling to be able to see a person's natural progression, particularly those who have been touched upon by the spirit. This is exactly what our work is about reaching out to people, extending welcoming arms and embracing them within the power that permeates this whole universe, the power of the spirit.

Chapter 13

It's been a long slow and yet successful ten years. In this time I have been able to master the techniques of being patient. Not being so amongst other things was one of my greatest downfalls. I have learned not only the purpose, but the truthfulness of our lives within this great world and how I operate as a person, within its' physical boundaries, boundaries that can be broken into limitless forms of positive energy and spiritual power.

After the great fall there has always been a soft landing, followed by words of wisdom from my teachers and guide, in the spirit world. Those dear people who have chosen to walk along the same path as I, always ready to welcome with warmth and love. I owe a great deal to them.

Daz has taught me many lessons in life. His sheer energy and beaming smile never fail to brighten even the most darkest of days. His determination and strength have often left me feeling somewhat inadequate and his personality has never failed to make me laugh. Daz always believes that he owes me a great deal for looking after him and despite the number of times I've told him, he has given to me a great sense of understanding much more than any amount of money could ever pay for, he still thinks this way. I shall have to sort him out!

Incidentally, we've just heard that Daz's foster sister has given birth to a beautiful baby girl, they've called her Melissa Jade. Daz is so thrilled to be an uncle again and I'm thrilled for all of them, the spirit world told us she would have a girl.

We also got a letter this morning from Hans and Annika Langlet. Annika was the Swedish lady who I'd given a test sitting to, whilst at Stansted Hall during the advanced mediumship week.

They've written to ask if I would like to go and visit their country and also do some work over there. Well, I'm not sure what to do, because I feel close enough to God as it is, without having to get on some plane and travel at thirty odd thousand feet.

Whatever the case, I'll certainly be sharing the experience with you all, till then, please be positive and peaceful knowing that you are being watched over by those you hold so dear to you, your people, your loved ones both here and in the spirit world......

My Loving Precious Mum

She Cannot bake a cake now nor can she shop alone, it's left a void so very deep within what was her home.

She wears her dresses all at once and tights are over shoes, it hurts so much to see my mum so tearful and confused.

We make a joke of everything to take her tears away, and point out errors we make too to brighten up her day.

She may not look as smart now this confused mum of mine, but still within her heart is a love I call divine.

I have to work so hard though on self to find a way, to keep me calm and patient God with me, please please stay.

Hands that took my hand before are hands that I now hold, I'll try to guide her onward and share her heavy load.

Her feet that always danced so can now just shuffle on, but never will the memory dim, of music, dance and song.

I'm so very lucky though painful it may be, because I know within my mum is a spirit that is free.

Free from what you may ask and I will tell you true, my mum is just the same within, the one I always knew.

Loving, caring friend and guide she held so many roles, I still am learning from her and try to make her goals.

Val Lacey

Information

further information about Paul Norton, his private and public meetings and other appearances can be obtained by sending a stamped, self addressed envelope to:

**PAUL NORTON
c/o LIVING WORLD PUBLICATIONS
PO BOX 177
DONCASTER
SOUTH YORKSHIRE
DN5 9XA**

Psychic World

'The independent voice of spiritualism'

A whole variety of topics and writers covering news, scientific aspects of spiritualism philosophy, views and other subjects.

for subscription details please write to

**PSYCHIC WORLD PUBLISHING CO LTD
22 KINGSLEY AVENUE
SOUTHALL
MIDDLESEX
UB1 2NA**